David R. Peterson
Nancy Schendel

An International Accounting Practice Set: The Karissa Jean's Simulation

Pre-publication REVIEWS, COMMENTARIES, EVALUATIONS . . .

"The authors do an extraordinary job of presenting a useful, easy-to-read guide for the beginning student in international accounting. Providing the students with the opportunity to perform the duties of an international accountant allows students to experience the interaction of foreign trade. The self-tests are an excellent tool for students to check themselves in their ability to comprehend the information presented in this book."

Geri A. Kahler, CPA
Staff Accountant,
Erpelding, Voigt, & Co., LLP

More pre-publication
REVIEWS, COMMENTARIES, EVALUATIONS . . .

"In the introductory section of the book, the authors present an excellent economic review of two much-needed topics: the international exchange rate and the balance of payments. With more and more U.S. companies becoming involved in international business, students need a more intense exposure to these topics than the usual perfunctory chapter inclusion.

I liked the well-placed examples and student progress tests which I believe will greatly assist the student's understanding of rather difficult subject material.

The text material and problem set engages the student in one continuous, interesting company selling a product that is easily recognized and to which a student might readily identify.

I highly recommend the practice set to instructors who would like their students to have a hands-on presentation of the complicated topic of international accounting."

Keith E. Wells, MBE
Assistant Professor,
University of New Mexico

"Karissa Jean's is an unusual practice set in that it provides a very good review of the accounting principles needed throughout the practice set at the beginning of the set. I feel that Karissa Jean's would be an excellent continuing professional education (CPE) course for CPAs who plan on dealing with international clients."

Ronald C. Hickman, CPA
General Manager,
Cycle Country Accessories Corp.,
Milford, Iowa

"The authors have done a wonderful job of making a complex subject understandable. This practice set should prove beneficial to students or accountants new to the international side of business. Especially useful were the thorough practice exams that will challenge the reader to immediately use their newly gained knowledge."

Mark D. Renze, MBA
International Business Analyst,
Nashville, Tennessee

International Business Press
An Imprint of The Haworth Press, Inc.

An International Accounting Practice Set
The Karissa Jean's Simulation

INTERNATIONAL BUSINESS PRESS
Erdener Kaynak, PhD
Executive Editor

New, Recent, and Forthcoming Titles:

An International Accounting Practice Set
The Karissa Jean's Simulation

David R. Peterson
Nancy Schendel

International Business Press
An Imprint of The Haworth Press, Inc.
New York • London

Published by

International Business Press, an imprint of The Haworth Press, Inc., 10 Alice Street, Binghamton, NY 13904-1580

Library of Congress Cataloging-in-Publication Data

Peterson, David R.
    An international accounting practice set : the Karissa Jean's Simulation / David R. Peterson, Nancy Schendel.
       p. cm
    Includes index.
    ISBN 0-7890-6021-3 (alk. paper).
    1. International business enterprises–Accounting. 2. Comparative accounting. 3. Accounting–Simulation methods. I. Schendel, Nancy. II. Title.
HF5686.I56P48 1996
657'.96–dc20
                                                 95-35021
                                                   CIP

Dedicated to two Beverlys:

For Beverly Peterson for 25 years of support.
Love,
Dave

In memory of Beverly Schendel.
Love,
Nancy

ABOUT THE AUTHORS

David R. Peterson, MBA, is Instructor of Business at Iowa Lakes Community College in Estherville, Iowa. He has 28 years of experience teaching business courses at community colleges and is the recipient of several national teaching awards. The author or co-author of 21 books primarily on business topics, Mr. Peterson has experience in a variety of business activities including real estate and insurance sales. He has also been a professional recording studio owner, specialty products distributor, and seminar presenter.

Nancy Schendel, CPA, MBA, is Accounting Specialist Coordinator at Iowa Lakes Community College in Estherville, Iowa. She has 12 years of teaching experience and three years of experience in public accounting. She regularly teaches courses in accounting principles, intermediate accounting, cost accounting, and auditing.

CONTENTS

Preface

An International Accounting Practice Set: The Karissa Jean's Simulation can be used by anyone who has completed one semester, or even one quarter, of accounting principles study.

You are to assume the role of a newly hired employee in the International Accounting Department of Karissa Jean's, an international distributor of men's and women's jeans. In this role, you will first participate in Karissa Jean's training program in international business and international accounting by completing the *Training Manual* portion of the practice set. Here, you will learn everything you need to know to complete the second part of the practice set, the *Simulation*. In the Simulation, you will perform as an international accountant in Karissa Jean's International Accounting Department. In addition to performing accounting activities, you will also gain experience in problem solving and writing.

The company utilized in this practice set–Karissa Jean's–is an international distributor of clothing products. The same international business and accounting principles and practices would be used by virtually any other international business regardless of the product they handle. Thus, if you become associated with a business that is engaged in international business selling electronics, furniture, hardware, appliances, sporting goods, musical instruments, office equipment, or whatever, the activities should be very similar to those performed by you for Karissa Jean's in this practice set.

Inter-Office Memo

Karissa Jean's®

To: Our Newest International
Accountant

From: Beverly Carter
International Accounting Department Manager

Subject: Welcome!

Date: January 11, 19—

Welcome to your first day at Karissa Jean's! We hope that today will be the beginning of a long and mutually beneficial relationship. All of us at Karissa Jean's, and particularly those of us in the International Accounting Department, will do our best to help you become acquainted with our company and our procedures.

Before you begin your day-to-day activities in the International Accounting Department, you will participate in Karissa Jean's training program. This program is designed to acquaint you with our company's background and operating philosophy and to familiarize you with the principles of international business and international accounting. After you have completed the training program, you will be assigned various international accounting duties.

Start by reading and studying the following material in Karissa Jean's Training Manual. If you have any questions, feel free to ask me or your immediate supervisor for assistance.

Welcome aboard—and, best wishes for a successful and enjoyable career at Karissa Jean's.

Karissa Jean's®

Training Manual

Chapter 1

Introduction

At Karissa Jean's we believe it is important that all employees understand how our company started and how it grew to become the international company it is today. This background will help you better understand company policies and the reasoning behind company decisions and practices.

Another purpose of this training program is to familiarize you with international business procedures, international accounting practices, and Karissa Jean's international accounting system.

THE ORIGIN OF KARISSA JEAN'S

In the fall of 1974, at age 18, Karissa Jean Fowler entered the University of Virginia to pursue a degree in elementary education. To support herself and to pay college expenses, Karissa worked 30 hours a week as a seamstress at a garment factory, Silver Threads. Silver Threads is a contract manufacturer, which sews garments for a variety of clothing companies according to their specifications. The clothing companies then market the garments under their own brand names to retailers, who in turn sell them to consumers.

Karissa took her job at Silver Threads seriously and decided to learn all that she could about the garment industry. After about a year, Karissa was promoted to Production Supervisor of her shift. At about that time, Karissa decided to make a career of the garment industry and changed her major to marketing. Karissa received several promotions at Silver Threads and worked in a variety of capacities for the company.

Karissa graduated from the University of Virginia in the spring of 1979. Her marketing degree and five years' experience in the garment industry enabled Karissa to land a job in the marketing department of Levi Strauss of San Francisco, a well-known and highly successful manufacturer of jeans and other clothing products.

Karissa had a successful career at Levi Strauss and was involved in developing marketing and promotional programs for the company's products for sale throughout the United States and, eventually, internationally.

Early in her career, Karissa developed the goal of one day owning her own garment company, probably manufacturing and selling jeans. Throughout her career at Levi Strauss, Karissa lived modestly and saved and invested her money, planning ahead to the day when she would start her company. In 1987, after nearly nine years in the marketing department at Levi Strauss, Karissa left the company to pursue her dream. Karissa was 31 years old at the time.

Karissa believed that she could locate her company anywhere in the United States and still have the same chance of being successful. She chose Denver, Colorado, because of its somewhat central location, relatively low rent and labor costs, and excellent transportation facilities. There were personal reasons, too. On her many business trips around the country for Levi Strauss, Karissa had fallen in love with the Denver area and the nearby Rocky Mountains and had decided that one day she would like to live there, if possible. Since she was now starting her own company, it was indeed possible. And, it turned out to be a good move.

Karissa obtained a three-year lease on office and warehouse facilities at 8677 Colfax Avenue. Next, Karissa hired two key employees, Jill Ryan as office manager, and Sean McMasters as sales manager. By this time Karissa's old friends at Silver Threads in Charlottesville, Virginia, had completed 500 samples of Karissa's new jean designs.

Karissa and Sean spent the next two months traveling the country, contacting purchasing agents for major department stores, chains, and catalog companies. The acceptance of Karissa Jean's line of jeans was outstanding.

By the end of 1987, orders for more than $1 million had been placed and Karissa Jean's was on its way to becoming a huge success in the garment industry.

By the end of 1990, annual sales reached $5 million in the United

States and Karissa Jean's decided to enter the international market. Karissa Jean's international business activities will be explained to you in detail after you read the forthcoming section on international business.

Karissa Jean's Jeans

Karissa began experimenting with clothing designs while a part-time employee at Silver Threads while attending college. She continued to study fabrics and experiment with designs during her years at Levi Strauss. By the time she left Levi Strauss to start her own company, Karissa had decided on an image for her jeans and had selected the proper fabric and design to project that image.

Karissa Jean's jeans have been positioned for the upscale designer market. The fabric is a tightly woven, slightly brushed denim that is just as strong and durable as that used for work jeans, yet the jeans are attractive enough to be worn for nearly any social occasion.

The jeans carry the distinctive Karissa Jean's logo on the back pocket and also on the front just below the waistband. This is the same logo that now appears on all of Karissa Jean's letterheads, invoices, and other printed materials.

Since the contour of the male body and the female body differ, Karissa decided to develop different patterns for each sex.

The result of this careful planning is a strong, durable, attractive jean with a great fit and prestige image.

Karissa Jean's does not own any manufacturing facilities or equipment. All of the manufacturing is done by contract manufacturers in the garment industry, with Silver Threads being the major supplier. Karissa Jean's main activities, then, are designing and marketing the jeans.

More About Karissa Jean's Later

Additional information about Karissa Jean's current business activities will be presented later in this training manual. But now, study the following information on international business and international accounting so you can better understand Karissa Jean's international operations when explained later in this training program.

Chapter 2

Understanding International Business

The United States' economy and the economies of other countries in the world are interdependent and are becoming more so all the time. A company that sells to or buys from a company or government in another country, or that operates in another country, is said to be engaged in *international business*.

A primary reason why business is becoming increasingly international in scope is that natural resources, economic resources, human resources, production capabilities, and consumption are not evenly distributed throughout the world. A country with an oversupply of a particular resource and that can produce that product at a lower cost than other countries, is said to have an *absolute advantage* over other countries. Some countries with limited resources may have no absolute advantage over other countries. Still, those countries can make some products more efficiently than others they produce. This is called a *comparative advantage*.

It makes good sense, then, for countries to manufacture products where they have an absolute advantage or comparative advantage, and to market them to the rest of the world. Profits earned from these sales are then used to buy products that are produced more efficiently in other countries.

Since no country has all of the resources and technology to produce all of the goods and services its people demand, all countries are involved in international trade.

BALANCE OF TRADE

Goods produced in one country and sold in another country are called *exports* of the producing country and *imports* of the consuming country. The difference between a country's exports and imports is called the *balance of trade*. If exports exceed imports, a *trade surplus* results; if imports exceed exports, it is a *trade deficit*. Obviously, each country seeks to obtain a favorable balance of trade, or trade surplus, since this provides jobs for its people and economic growth for its country.

The United States traditionally has its greatest volume of both exports and imports with Canada, Japan, and Mexico, in that order. Prior to 1970, the United States had a trade surplus each year. Since 1970, however, the United States has had a trade surplus only three years, all of which were in the early 1970s. The United States has had a huge annual trade deficit with Japan and also has large trade deficits with Saudi Arabia, Taiwan, China, Africa, Venezuela, and several other countries. Although the United States has annual trade deficits with both Canada and Mexico, they are small in comparison to some of the other countries. The United States has an annual trade surplus with only a handful of countries, including Australia, the United Kingdom, France, and Spain.

United States' exports exceed imports of agricultural products, chemicals, aerospace, aircraft, and services. United States' imports exceed exports of motor vehicles, petroleum, electronics, consumer goods, and machinery.

BALANCE OF PAYMENTS

Another measure of international business activity is the *balance of payments*, which is the difference between *all* payments made to and receipts received from foreign countries and their residents. The balance of payments includes goods (the balance of trade) plus services, purchases made by tourists, transportation purchased on foreign carriers, investments made in foreign countries, gifts given to foreign residents and interest and dividends paid to foreign investors. Since the balance of trade has a strong effect on the balance of payments, the United States has had a negative balance of payments most years since 1970.

WAYS TO ENTER FOREIGN MARKETS

There are several basic ways in which a company can enter a foreign market. These vary considerably in the amount of investment, expertise, and long-term commitment required, in the risk involved, and in the profit potential.

Generally, the methods which require the greatest investment in the foreign country offer the greatest potential for profit, but also hold the greatest financial risk if difficulties arise.

Exporting

The easiest, least expensive, and least risky way for a company to enter a foreign market is to manufacture its goods in its domestic plant and to export them to the foreign country for sale. This requires no investment in foreign facilities and creates jobs, profit, and economic growth in the domestic country. Profits might be limited, however, because of high production and transportation costs, because local companies in the foreign country may be able to produce competing goods at a lower cost, and because foreign governments may impose taxes and restrictions on imported goods. There are two exporting methods available for use: *direct exporting* and *indirect exporting*.

Direct Exporting

When a company uses *direct exporting*, it locates wholesalers and distributors in the foreign country and sells its goods directly to them. The wholesalers and distributors then resell the goods to businesses or individuals in their country. The exporting company handles all details of the sale including the calculation of taxes and duties, conversion of currency, and shipping arrangements. Thus, the exporting company needs to become knowledgeable about each country's import regulations and business practices that it exports to.

Indirect Exporting

When a company uses *indirect exporting*, the company engages an export management company in its own country to handle the sale of goods to foreign countries. Some export management companies take title to the goods and sell them to wholesalers in foreign countries. Others act as an agent of the exporting company, selling the company's goods to foreign customers and collecting a sales commission from the exporting company. In either case, the export management company takes care of all details involved in exportation.

The advantages of using the indirect exporting method are first, the exporting company doesn't need to develop any expertise in export procedures and regulations and second, the export management company can provide an instant market for the company's goods. The disadvantages are: charges for the export management company's services can be high, sales results can be sporadic and disappointing, and the exporting company fails to develop its own expertise in exporting its goods.

Many companies enter exporting by using indirect exporting because it is so easy to use, but eventually shift to direct exporting when they develop more knowledge and expertise in exporting procedures.

Licensing

A company that owns valuable rights, such as patents, copyrights, trademarks, trade names, manufacturing processes, or marketing procedures can earn money by *licensing* these rights to a company in a foreign country. The foreign company, the *licensee*, then makes all of the investment required and uses the right or procedure to operate its business in that country. The licensee usually pays the owner of the right, the *licensor*, a fee when the licensing agreement is signed and also pays a royalty, perhaps 2 percent to 5 percent, on all sales it makes during the licensing period.

The licensing period extends for a specific time, such as five years, and often the licensee has the option of renewing the license.

For a company with valuable rights, licensing can be an inexpensive, easy, and risk-free way to earn substantial profits. For the licensee, it is an opportunity to increase the probability of success by using existing technology and procedures that have a proven track record.

Of course, licensing also has potential disadvantages for the licensor. For instance, if the licensee fails to make a profit, they may be unable to pay the licensor's royalty. Also, after the license expires, the licensee may use the knowledge and expertise learned from the licensor to become a direct competitor of the licensor. For this reason, many companies view licensing as a shortsighted approach to entering foreign markets and refuse to get involved in licensing agreements. They prefer to market their products in foreign countries themselves using one of the other methods available.

Franchising

Franchising is a form of licensing whereby a business operator, the *franchisor*, who has a highly recognizable name and a successful business formula contracts with a person or company, the *franchisee*, to allow them to operate a business according to the franchisor's plan.

The franchise provides the franchisor with greater protection than the usual licensing arrangement since the franchisor can require that its procedures be followed and its standards be met. A franchisor has greater costs than a licensor, however, since the franchisor provides training and advisors to the franchisee. It also must monitor the franchisee's activities to ensure than the franchisor's business plan is being followed.

In return for use of its name and business procedures and for the assistance provided, the franchisor receives a franchise fee plus a royalty on sales made by the franchisee.

Joint Venture

A company can enter a foreign market by forming a *joint venture*, or partnership, with a company in that foreign country. Together, they manufacture and/or market products in that country.

The domestic company in that foreign country contributes guidance on local customs and culture and on marketing the goods. It may also provide facilities, human resources, and a distribution system. The foreign company contributes technological know-how, management expertise, and financial investment.

An advantage of the joint venture is that by working together and pooling resources and capabilities, the two companies can enter a market that neither may have been able to manage by themselves.

On the negative side, all partnerships are laden with potential problems. This is magnified when dealing with a partner from a different culture who may have an incompatible perspective of how business should be conducted. Because of this potential incompatibility, many United States companies are reluctant to form a joint venture with a foreign company. Some governments, however, require that foreign companies who want to own a business in their land must have local investors involved in the venture. Thus, foreign companies that want to own and operate manufacturing facilities in that country are virtually forced into a joint venture.

Marketing Subsidiary

Another way for a company to sell its products in a foreign country is to establish a *marketing subsidiary* in that country. Here, the company establishes a distribution center and staffs it with local employees. The company sends a few of its own employees to the foreign country to manage and supervise the distribution center. The company then ships its products to the distribution center, which markets the product throughout the country.

Insufficient knowledge of local marketing techniques, a lack of contacts, and unfamiliarity with the local culture often make it very difficult for an American company to establish an effective distribution system in a foreign country. Therefore, relatively few United States companies establish their own marketing subsidiaries in foreign countries.

Contract Manufacturer

A company can get its products manufactured in a foreign country by contracting with a local manufacturer, known as a *contract manufacturer*, to produce the goods according to its specifications. The company then markets the products itself through its own sales organization or through a marketing subsidiary.

The use of contract manufacturers eliminates the cost and problems of investing in production facilities in the foreign country. It may also result in savings in costs for labor, shipping, and import duties compared to manufacturing the goods in the company's domestic country.

Potential problems may include the difficulty in monitoring the production process to be certain that goods adhere to the company's standards.

Wholly Owned Subsidiary

Many companies prefer to enter a foreign market by building a new manufacturing plant or by buying an existing plant in that country. This total ownership of facilities in a foreign country is known as a *wholly owned subsidiary.*

Many companies prefer a wholly owned subsidiary to a joint venture since there is no foreign partner to deal with or to share profits with. Many foreign governments also like the wholly owned subsidiary since it creates investment and employment in their country. In fact, many foreign governments offer tax breaks and other incentives to encourage such investment.

Of all the methods of entering a foreign market, operating a wholly owned subsidiary can be the most profitable. It also requires the greatest investment and holds the greatest risks, however. For instance, there may be difficulty adapting to the culture and customs in that country as well as in supervising a local labor force.

Then, too, there is no guarantee that the business will be successful and if it should fail, the company could be stuck with facilities it cannot sell. Also, if the foreign government changes its policies, it could become difficult or impossible to operate in that country.

PROGRESS TEST 1

This self-test is presented to allow you to measure your comprehension of the material about the origination of Karissa Jean's and international trade presented so far in this training manual. After you have completed this self-test, compare your answers to those found in the back of this manual. Use the following grading scale to evaluate your comprehension of this material and to determine what to do next.

Points Correct	Evaluation
14-15	*Excellent!* You have studied this section of the training manual thoroughly. Proceed to the next section. Keep up the good work!
12-13	*Good!* You have a good command of the information presented. Quickly review the areas you missed and then proceed to the next section.
10-11	*Fair.* A more serious effort is required on your part. Thoroughly review the preceding section before continuing.
Below 10	*Poor.* You must devote more time and effort to studying this training manual or you will be incompetent to perform your duties at Karissa Jean's. Go back to the beginning and start over before continuing.

1. The complete name of the founder of Karissa Jean's is (A) Karissa Ann Fowler (B) Karissa Jean McMasters (C) Karissa Jean Ryan (D) Karissa Jean Fowler

2. While attending college at the University of Virginia, Karissa worked part-time in a/an _____ factory. (A) Auto (B) Garment (C) Shoe (D) Computer

3. After graduation from college, Karissa obtained a position in the marketing department of what company? (A) Calvin Klein (B) Gloria Vanderbilt (C) Levi Strauss (D) Wrangler

4. A company with an oversupply of a particular resource that can produce that product at a lower cost than other countries is said to have a/an _____ over other countries. (A) Marginal Advantage (B) Comparative Advantage (C) Absolute Advantage (D) Dominated Advantage

5. Goods produced in one country and sold to another country are called a/an _____ of the producing country and a/an

_____ of the consuming country. (A) Trade Surplus-Trade Deficit (B) Balance of Trade-Balance of Payment (C) Export-Import (D) Import-Export

6. The difference between a company's exports and its imports is called the _____. (A) Balance of Trade (B) Balance of Payments (C) Trade Surplus (D) Comparative Advantage

7. When a company's exports exceed its imports, a/an _____ results. (A) Absolute Advantage (B) Trade Surplus (C) Comparative Balance of Trade (D) Trade Deficit

8. When a company that owns valuable rights, such as patents, trade names, or manufacturing processes, allows a foreign company to use these rights to conduct their business using their own methods, it is called _____. (A) Franchising (B) Licensing (C) Indirect Exporting (D) A Marketing Subsidiary

9. A company that establishes a distribution center in a foreign country and that staffs it with mostly local employees to market the company's goods has established a/an _____. (A) Wholly Owned Subsidiary (B) Joint Venture (C) Licensing Arrangement (D) Marketing Subsidiary

10. When a company locates wholesalers and distributors in a foreign country and sells its goods directly to those wholesalers and distributors, it is engaged in _____. (A) Licensing (B) Direct Exporting (C) Indirect Exporting (D) Franchising

11. When a company enters a foreign market by building a new manufacturing plant or buying an existing plant in that country, it has established a/an _____. (A) Wholly Owned Subsidiary (B) Marketing Subsidiary (C) Joint Venture (D) Franchise Arrangement

12. A partnership formed with a company in a foreign country for the purpose of conducting business in that country is called a/an _____. (A) Contract Manufacturing Arrangement (B) Licensing Arrangement (C) Joint Venture (D) Jointly Owned Subsidiary

13. When a company engages an export management company in its own country to handle the sale of its goods to foreign countries, it is engaged in _____. (A) Licensing (B) Direct Exporting (C) A Marketing Subsidiary (D) Indirect Exporting

14. The easiest, least expensive, and least risky way for a company to enter a foreign market is to do so through: (A) A Wholly Owned Subsidiary (B) Exporting (C) A Marketing Subsidiary (D) A Joint Venture

15. Companies such as Silver Threads, that manufacture Karissa Jean's jeans according to Karissa Jean's specifications, are called _____. (A) Contract Manufacturers (B) Joint Ventures (C) Marketing Subsidiaries (D) Licensees

Chapter 3

Obstacles to International Trade

Operating in international trade can be very complex and difficult because of differences in customs, cultures, language, currencies, government policies, and economic conditions between countries. Also, many governments seek to protect their domestic companies from foreign competitors and therefore impose many restrictions on foreign companies and place many barriers in their way. Some of these obstacles to operating in international trade are briefly described below.

CULTURAL DIFFERENCES

Each country has its own customs, values, religions, and attitudes which must be understood and complied with in order to successfully conduct business in that country. Inadequate knowledge of a country's culture can result in serious misunderstandings and lost sales or even complete business failure.

LANGUAGE DIFFERENCES

Many English words and phrases, when translated into foreign languages, result in inaccuracies or embarrassing connotations. Thus, a thorough knowledge of the foreign country's language and culture are needed when naming products, developing advertising slogans, and making translations.

Additional language problems may arise when selling goods in a country such as Canada that has two dominant languages, English and French. The Canadian government requires that products be labeled in both languages. This poses not only an interpretation problem but also a problem in designing a label large enough to carry both languages and small enough to fit on the package. In other countries, even if the local language or dual languages are not required, it may be a wise marketing decision to use this labeling procedure anyway to show that country's residents you understand and honor their culture.

ECONOMIC CONDITIONS

Economic conditions vary dramatically from one country to another. In a small, densely populated country such as Japan, for instance, land and building costs may be ten times or more that of a comparable site in New York City, perhaps making it unfeasible to buy or build facilities there.

In poorer countries, people may have so little money that they cannot buy anything but basic necessities. And, customary American packaging of goods by the pack, six-pack, case, or jumbo box may be too large a quantity for them to afford at one time.

Some countries, in recent years, have had annual inflation rates of 1,000 percent, 20,000 percent, or more. This, of course, makes it extremely difficult to buy materials and supplies, to price goods, and to plan ahead. Many companies, however, employ a process known as *hedging* to buy materials for future delivery to help combat the problems of inflation.

In some countries, the basic currency unit has become worth very little because of inflation and other factors. For instance, on one particular day, one American dollar was worth 12,507 Polish zloty or 3,116 Mexican pesos.

Sometimes to get the currency to a more manageable number, the country will *devalue* its currency by decreasing the number of currency units it takes to equal an American dollar. In January, 1993, for instance, Mexico devalued the peso by creating a new peso equal to 1,000 old pesos. No gain or loss was experienced on the devaluation since after devaluation it took 3,120 old pesos ($) or 3.12 new pesos ($N) to equal one American dollar.

MARKETING DIFFICULTIES

In many countries, data on population size, consumer interests, market size, and the like is either unavailable or is highly inaccurate. This makes it extremely difficult for a foreign company to gather market information, to conduct market research, and to make sales projections.

The *infrastructure* (communications and transportation systems) of many countries is far inferior to that in the United States. For instance, in some countries it may take hours to get a telephone line, and when you do get one, you may get cut off in the middle of your conversation. This, of course, makes it very difficult to locate and negotiate with potential business clients. Likewise, poor transportation routes and equipment make it difficult to ship goods when and where you want them.

Then, too, in many countries, there may be no clearly established marketing channels for some goods, making it difficult to get your goods into the hands of consumers.

FLUCTUATING CURRENCY EXCHANGE RATES

Each country has its own currency such as the British pound, Mexican peso, Japanese yen, French franc, Italian lira, and American dollar. These currencies are not of equal value. Therefore, each day, *currency exchange rates* are quoted that show the value of each currency in terms of United States dollars. For instance, on a particular day, an American dollar equaled 123.80 Japanese yen, .6538 British pounds, or 1,376 Italian lira.

The American dollar is the common unit for which other currencies are usually exchanged. Although it is possible to convert from one country's currency to another country's currency, currencies are usually first converted to American dollars and then the dollars are converted to the next foreign currency. Thus, to convert from the Italian lira to the Japanese yen, lira are first converted to American dollars and then dollars are converted to yen.

The exchange rate between a country's currency and the United States dollar fluctuates daily. Factors that affect the exchange rate include inflation rates in the two countries, political changes, government policies, trade policies, and financial and business forecasts.

When a company in one country extends credit to a company in another country, calling for payment at a future date, an exchange rate risk exists since the exchange rate might fluctuate during the credit period. For instance, if an American company sells goods to a Japanese company, with payment to be made in dollars, the Japanese company assumes the risk that the value of yen may drop before the payment date. It will then take more yen to buy the specified number of dollars. On the other hand, if payment was to be made in yen and the value of yen drops, the American company would receive less when the yen it receives is converted to dollars.

The terms, *strong dollar* and *weak dollar* are often used when comparing the relative value of the American dollar to other countries' currencies. A strong dollar means that an American dollar can be exchanged for more of a foreign currency and that an American dollar will purchase more goods in a foreign country. A weak dollar means the opposite—an American dollar can be exchanged for less of a foreign currency and an American dollar will purchase less of a foreign country's goods.

When the American dollar is strong, Americans can buy more for their money in foreign markets and United States' imports increase. Likewise, a strong dollar means that American products are more costly for foreigners to buy and United States exports decline. Conversely, when the American dollar is weak, Americans find foreign goods to be expensive and a dollar will buy less. Thus, United States imports of foreign goods decrease. At the same time, a weak dollar results in less costly American goods for foreign buyers and United States' exports increase.

As you can see, fluctuating exchange rates between the American dollar and foreign currencies can greatly influence trade between the United States and other countries.

GOVERNMENT INSTABILITY

Governments and political systems of some countries are very unstable. A coup of political leaders, a revolution, a drastic change in foreign policy, or similar changes can dramatically affect the business climate in those countries. In times of drastic upheaval, some countries have taken over foreign firms operating on their soil without paying for them. This is known as *expropriation without reimbursement.*

Many foreign companies have lessened the chances of expropriation by being good and valuable corporate citizens, training and hiring domestic employees and remaining neutral in domestic affairs.

TRADE PROTECTIONISM

Governments often take steps to protect their domestic industries and companies from foreign competitors so their domestic companies can survive and, in fact, thrive. In theory, this *trade protectionism* protects domestic industries and saves companies as well as saves jobs.

In some cases, trade protectionism is justified to protect domestic companies that manufacture products vital to national defense. It is also often necessary to provide temporary protection to allow a fledgling industry to mature before being onslaught with foreign competitors.

In many cases, however, trade protectionism results from heavy lobbying from a special interest group or specific industry. Often, the protectionism protects that group or industry, but the entire country suffers by paying higher prices or by having limited offerings available. Then, too, trade protectionism instituted by one country often results in retaliation from a foreign country that places restrictions on the import of the other country's goods. The result is a trade war that hurts everyone.

Trade protectionism instituted by foreign governments can make it very difficult or impossible to conduct business within that country. Following are some of the more common types of trade protectionism.

Import Quotas

A country often limits the quantity of specific goods that can be imported, such as automobiles or wine. This is known as an *import quota.* Sometimes, an importing country can convince an exporting country to voluntarily limit its exports in return for a voluntary limit on goods it sells in the exporting country. Often, a country will voluntarily limit its exports because of fear of retaliation if it does not do so.

Taxes

Many countries impose a tax on imported goods, called a *tariff.* *Protective tariffs* are imposed to force the foreign exporter to raise its prices (to cover this additional tax). This makes the imported goods more expensive compared to domestically produced goods. Therefore, the country's residents will be more likely to buy the less expensive domestic products. *Revenue tariffs* are often imposed by developing countries as a method of generating revenue for its government.

Most countries welcome investment in new factories and production facilities in their country by foreign companies. However, they do not like to see the profits transferred back to the company's home country, known as *repatriation.* Therefore, many countries tax repatriation of profits heavily or forbid repatriation altogether. Therefore, a company might seek a more cooperative foreign country in which to locate its facilities or consider a different method of operating within that country.

Embargoes

An *embargo* prohibits a certain type of goods from being imported into a country or from being exported from the country.

Sometimes, *import embargoes* are placed on goods, such as livestock or foods, to protect the health of the country's people. In other cases, an import embargo may be placed on all goods of another country because the two countries have political differences or are feuding. This has the effect of weakening the exporting country's economy.

An *export embargo* might be placed on a country's own goods to preserve scarce natural resources or to safeguard technology or equipment.

Export Subsidies

Some governments make direct or indirect payments, known as *export subsidies,* to their domestic companies involved in exporting goods. These payments may be monetary, or they may be in the form of tax credits or low interest rate loans. An export subsidy allows the exporting company to sell its products at a lower price in foreign markets and still earn a profit.

This makes it difficult for companies in the importing country to compete with the foreign goods in their domestic market. It also makes it virtually impossible for companies to compete in the world market against a foreign company receiving the export subsidy. Even though many countries pay export subsidies, it is considered an unethical business practice.

Companies that receive export subsidies are in an excellent position to engage in an unethical practice known as dumping. *Dumping* is the selling of exported goods at a price below their cost or below what they sell at in the exporter's country. These cheap goods can drive domestic companies in the importing country out of business and the exporting company can then monopolize sales in that country.

If a domestic industry can convince its government that dumping is taking place, the government will usually retaliate by imposing import quotas or tariffs, or take other measures to protect its domestic companies.

Retaliation

If the government of one country raises tariffs, lowers import quotas, or takes other measures to decrease imports, the government of an affected exporting country may take similar steps to retaliate. While the two countries are locked in a power struggle, individual companies in both countries suffer because of lost exports.

OVERCOMING INTERNATIONAL TRADE OBSTACLES

As you can see, there are many potential barriers to becoming involved in international trade. However, the huge profit potential that exists in international trade often makes it worthwhile to find ways to overcome these obstacles.

The United States Department of Commerce, various federal government agencies, and state government agencies are eager to provide information and assistance about how to best enter international trade. This information and assistance can help avoid grave errors and can help overcome the many potential obstacles to international trade.

Chapter 4

International Trade Organizations

Numerous trade organizations have been formed to foster international trade, to protect the rights of member countries and/or to settle trade disputes. Membership in these organizations fluctuates from time to time, as countries find it advantageous to join or leave an organization. The following are representative of the many, and more prominent, international trade organizations.

GENERAL AGREEMENT ON TARIFFS AND TRADE (GATT)

The *General Agreement on Tariffs and Trade* (GATT) is a treaty signed in 1947 to stimulate international trade and to establish a procedure for settling trade disputes between member countries. Over 100 countries now belong to GATT and member countries account for over 80 percent of international trade. GATT has been particularly successful in settling trade disputes and in lowering tariffs on numerous goods.

INTERNATIONAL MONETARY FUND (IMF)

The *International Monetary Fund* (IMF) was established in 1944 to stabilize exchange rates of currencies of member countries and to establish an orderly system for making currency exchanges.

THE WORLD BANK

The World Bank, owned jointly by over 120 countries, provides less-developed countries with funds for economic development and to help further their international trade. The World Bank borrows money from wealthier countries and lends it to developing countries at current interest rates. Many companies have found that countries with a new loan from The World Bank are excellent potential customers since they now have funds available for international trade.

ECONOMIC COMMUNITIES

Groups of countries with similarities and common interests that join together to form trade alliances are called *economic communities*.

The most successful economic community is the *European Community* (EC), which is also sometimes called the European Economic Community (EEC) or the Common Market (CM). The European Community was established in 1958 and now consists of the following 12 countries: Belgium, Denmark, France, Germany, Greece, Ireland, Italy, Luxembourg, Netherlands, Portugal, Spain, and the United Kingdom. The European Community has abolished all tariffs and trade restrictions on trade among member countries and a uniform tariff has been established between members of the EC and nonmember countries.

The European Community has provided great trade benefits for its 12 members and has afforded great trade opportunities for foreign companies with facilities in one of these countries.

Other prominent economic communities include the *Central American Common Market* (El Salvador, Nicaragua, Guatemala, and Costa Rica), the *Latin American Integration Association* (Argentina, Bolivia, Brazil, Chile, Colombia, Ecuador, Mexico, Paraguay, Peru, Uruguay, and Venezuela), and the *European Free Trade Association* (Austria, Finland, Iceland, Norway, Sweden, and Switzerland).

None of these economic communities have been able to establish the degree of cooperation of free trade found in the European Community. This is partly because of the political and economic diversity found in member countries.

CARTELS

A *cartel* is an organization of countries that produce a raw material or commodity such as petroleum, coffee, sugar, or rubber and which controls the supply and prices of these materials. The best known cartel is the *Organization of Petroleum Exporting Countries* (OPEC). Members include the oil-producing countries of Abu Dhabi, Algeria, Ecuador, Gabon, Indonesia, Iran, Iraq, Kuwait, Libya, Qatar, Saudi Arabia, and Venezuela.

OPEC was highly effective in controlling production and in raising prices in the 1970s. By 1980, the price of a barrel of crude oil was more than ten times the 1970 price. This resulted in high inflation, recession, and unemployment in major oil-importing countries such as the United States.

It also resulted in steps by oil-importing countries to find ways to reduce consumption by conserving energy and by finding alternative energy sources such as wind power and solar power. These countries also sought to increase their own oil production through increased exploration for new oil deposits on their own soil.

This, in turn, resulted in decreased purchases of oil from OPEC countries. As the demand for oil decreased, some OPEC countries refused to cut production, since they did not want to decrease their income. This resulted in a surplus of petroleum on the market and by the mid-1980s oil prices fell to about one-third the 1980 level.

Predictably, the decrease in petroleum prices from OPEC countries has resulted in a disregard for conservation measures, an abandonment of the search for alternative energy sources, and a decrease in oil exploration by oil-importing countries. It is feared by some that this lackadaisical attitude may allow OPEC to regain its stranglehold on oil prices. If that occurs, American businesses may once again be faced with the problems caused by high energy costs—inflation, recession, and lay-offs of workers.

PROGRESS TEST 2

This self-test is presented to allow you to measure your comprehension of the material presented since Progress Test 1, *Obstacles to International Trade*, and *International Trade Organizations*. After you have completed this self-test, compare your answers to those found in the back of this manual. Use the following rating scale to evaluate your comprehension of this material and to determine what to do next.

Points Correct	*Evaluation*
14-15	*Excellent!* You have studied this section of the training manual thoroughly. Proceed to the next section. Keep up the good work!
12-13	*Good!* You have a good command of the information presented. Quickly review the areas you missed and then proceed to the next section.
10-11	*Fair.* A more serious effort is required on your part. Thoroughly review the preceding section before continuing.
Below 10	*Poor.* You *must* devote more time and effort to studying this training manual or you will be incompetent to perform your duties at Karissa Jean's. Go back to the beginning of this section and start over before continuing.

1. High inflation rates and a shortage of spendable money by a country's people are obstacles to international trade known as: (A) Government Stability (B) Cultural Differences (C) Trade Protectionism (D) Economic Conditions

2. Differences in customs, values, religions, and attitudes found in another country, which may cause an obstacle to international trade are called _____. (A) Economic Conditions (B) Cultural Differences (C) Marketing Differences (D) Trade Protectionism

3. When an American dollar can be exchanged for more of a foreign currency and can buy more goods in a foreign country than before, it is called a/an _____. (A) Weak Dollar (B) Strong Dollar (C) Trade Surplus (D) Expropriation

4. Quotations that show the value of foreign currencies in terms of United States dollars are called _____. (A) Expropriations (B) Revenue Tariffs (C) Exchange Rates (D) Currency Cartels

5. Steps taken by governments to protect their domestic industries and companies from foreign competitors so their domestic companies can survive are, in general, called _____. (A) Trade Protectionism (B) Cartels (C) Trade Barriers (D) Repatriation

6. When a country takes over foreign firms operating on its soil without paying for them, it is called _____. (A) Repatriation (B) A Cartel (C) Expropriation Without Reimbursement (D) Dumping

7. A tax imposed on imported goods, thus forcing the retail price of those goods to be raised, is called a/an _____. (A) Embargo (B) Import Quota (C) Repatriation (D) Tariff

8. A restriction which prohibits certain types of goods from being imported into a country or from being exported from a country is called a/an _____. (A) Tariff (B) Quota (C) Embargo (D) Retaliation

9. The transferring of profits in a foreign country back to the company's home country is called _____. (A) Expropriation (B) Retaliation (C) Repatriation (D) Export Subsidation

10. Direct or indirect payments by a government to its domestic companies involved in exporting goods, thereby allowing the companies to sell the goods at a lower price in foreign markets and still make a profit, is called _____. (A) Dumping (B) An Export Subsidy (C) An Export Embargo (D) Expropriation With Reimbursement

11. An organization of countries that produce a raw material and which controls the supply and prices of those materials is called a/an _____. (A) Embargo (B) Tariff (C) Export Quota (D) Cartel

12. Groups of countries with similarities and common interests that join together to form trade alliances are called _____. (A) Economic Communities (B) Cartels (C) Trade Protectionist Alliances (D) Central Markets

13. The 12 European countries that have joined together to form a trade alliance, including France, Germany, Denmark, Spain, and the United Kingdom are called the _____. (A) European Free Trade Association (B) European Community (C) European Trade Alliance (D) Central European Market

14. A limit placed by a country on the quantity of specific goods that can be imported into its country is called a/an _____. (A) Export Quota (B) Import Embargo (C) Import Quota (D) Marginal Import Limit

15. The process of selling exported goods at a price below their cost or below what they sell at in the exporter's country and thus driving domestic companies in the importing country out of business is called _____. (A) Dumping (B) Export Subordination (C) Plastering (D) An Export Tariff Buster

Chapter 5

International Accounting Practices

Any business engaged in international trade will also become involved in international accounting. In the United States, all international accounting activities must meet the guidelines set by the Financial Accounting Standards Board Statement No. 52 (FASB-52). FASB-52 includes guidelines for virtually every international accounting procedure imaginable. This training manual, however, includes only the FASB-52 guidelines that you will need to know to perform your duties at Karissa Jean's.

Recording financial transactions and converting foreign financial statements to terms of American dollars are the most common international accounting activities. In order to perform these activities, you will also need to understand currency exchange rates.

CURRENCY EXCHANGE RATES

As previously described in this training manual, the *currency exchange rate* is the value of a country's currency expressed in terms of another country's currency. Recall that the American dollar is the common unit for which other currencies of the world are exchanged.

The following table is typical of that found in financial publications worldwide on a daily basis. Notice that the quotations show foreign currency in dollars and dollars in foreign currencies for two consecutive days.

The *Foreign Currency in Dollars* means the number of American

CURRENCY EXCHANGE RATES
NEW YORK N.Y. – Foreign Exchange, New York prices.

	Foreign Currency In Dollars (Direct Quote)		Dollar in Foreign Currency (Indirect Quote)	
	Wed.	Tue.	Wed.	Tue.
Australia (dollar)	.6885	.6845	1.4524	1.4609
Austria (shilling)	.0894	.0888	11.184	11.265
Britain (pound)	1.5295	1.5180	.6538	.6588
Canada (dollar)	.7788	.7756	1.2840	1.2893
France (franc)	.1857	.1841	5.3860	5.4320
Germany (mark)	.6289	.6246	1.5900	1.6010
Hong Kong (dollar) ..	.1293	.1293	7.7330	7.7360
Italy (lira)	.000727	.000720	1376.00	1389.00
Japan (yen)	.008078	.008061	123.80	124.05
Mexico (peso)	.321	.321	3.118	3.118
So. Africa (rand)	.3320	.3317	3.0120	3.0148
Spain (peseta)	.008850	.008669	113.00	115.35
Switzerland (franc) ..	.7003	.6957	1.4280	1.4375

dollars it takes to buy one unit of the foreign currency. For instance, on Wednesday, it takes 1.5295 American dollars ($1.5295) to buy one British pound or .1857 American dollars ($.1857) to buy one French franc. This is called the *direct quote*.

The *Dollar in Foreign Currency* means the number of foreign currency units it takes to buy one American dollar. For example, on Wednesday, it takes .6538 British pounds or 1,376.00 Italian liras to buy one American dollar. This is called the *indirect quote*.

To convert a foreign currency to American dollars, American dollars to a foreign currency, or one foreign currency to another foreign currency, follow the procedures shown in the following examples.

Example 1: Converting Foreign Currency to American Dollars

To convert from various foreign currencies to American dollars, using the Wednesday exchange rates in the table above, use the direct quote and the procedure shown on the following page:

			Procedure				
Converted from Foreign Currency		=	Converted to American Dollars	Foreign Currency Amount	×	Direct Quote	=	American Dollars
50,000	British pounds	=	$76,475.00	50,000	×	1.5295	=	$76,475.00
25,000	French francs	=	$4,642.50	25,000	×	.1857	=	$4,642.50
40,000	German marks	=	$25,156.00	40,000	×	.6289	=	$25,156.00
200,000	Italian lira	=	$145.40	200,000	×	.000727	=	$145.40
30,000	Swiss francs	=	21,009.00	30,000	×	.7003	=	$21,009.00

Example 2: Converting American Dollars to Foreign Currencies

To convert from American dollars to various foreign currencies using the Wednesday exchange rates in the preceding table, use the indirect quote and the procedure shown below:

Converted from American Dollars	Converted to Foreign Currency		American Dollars	×	Indirect Quote	=	Foreign Currency Amount
$20,000	13,076.00	British pounds	$20,000	×	.6538	=	13,076.00
$50,000	269,300.00	French francs	$50,000	×	5.3860	=	269,300.00
$15,000	115,995.00	Hong Kong dollars	$15,000	×	7.7330	=	115,995.00
$12,000	1,485,600.00	Japanese yen	$12,000	×	123.80	=	1,485,600.00
$5,000	15,590.00	Mexican pesos	$5,000	×	3.118	=	15,590.00

Example 3: Converting from One Foreign Currency to Another

It is possible to convert directly from one foreign currency to another, if the proper exchange rates are available. Usually, however, the foreign currency is first converted to American dollars using the direct quote and then the American dollars are converted to the foreign currency using the indirect quote, as shown below. The exchange rates used are those for Wednesday found in the preceding table.

Converted from Foreign Currency		=	Converted to Foreign Currency		Procedure
2,000	British pounds	=	16,475.77	French francs	*Step 1*—Convert pounds to dollars 2,000 × 1.5295 = $3,059.00
					Step 2—Convert dollars to francs $3,059.00 × 5.3860 = 16,475.77
6,000,000	Japanese yen	=	77,064.12	German marks	*Step 1*—Convert yen to dollars 6,000,000 × .008078 = $48,468.00
					Step 2—Convert dollars to marks $48,468.00 × 1.5900 = 77,064.12
4,000	British pounds	=	8,418,368.00	Italian liras	*Step 1*—Convert pounds to dollars 4,000 × 1.5295 = $6,118.00
					Step 2—Convert dollars to liras $6,118.00 × 1376.00 = 8,418,368.00

Practice Problems: Currency Exchange Rates

The currency exchange rates shown on p. 33 were taken from a financial publication dated about two weeks after the exchange

CURRENCY EXCHANGE RATES
NEW YORK, N.Y. – Foreign Exchange, New York prices.

	Foreign Currency In Dollars (Direct Quote)		Dollar in Foreign Currency (Indirect Quote)	
	Tue.	Wed.	Tue.	Wed.
Australia (dollar)	.6930	.6915	1.4430	1.4461
Austria (shilling)	.0913	.0910	10.950	10.985
Britain (pound)	1.5955	1.5970	.6268	.6262
Canada (dollar)	.7860	.7851	1.2722	1.2738
Denmark (kroner) . .	.1662	.1633	6.0165	6.1255
France (franc)	.1884	.1882	5.3070	5.3145
Germany (mark)	.6423	.6414	1.5570	1.5590
Hong Kong (dollar) . .	.1291	.1291	7.7440	7.7450
Italy (lira)	.000728	.000727	1374.00	1375.50
Japan (yen)	.008068	.008071	123.95	123.90
Mexico (peso)	.321	.321	3.115	3.112
So. Africa (rand)	.3356	.3331	2.9800	3.0020
Spain (peseta)	.008985	.008826	111.30	113.30
Switzerland (franc) . .	.7168	.7174	1.3950	1.3940

rates shown in the preceding examples. Notice that the exchange rates have fluctuated during this two-week period.

Use the Tuesday prices from the exchange rates shown above to make the following currency conversions. After you have completed your work, refer to the answers at the back of this training manual to check your answers and to verify your procedures.

	Converted from Foreign Currency		=	Converted to American Dollars	Procedure
1.	15,000	Canadian dollars	=	$	
2.	250,000	Japanese yen	=	$	
3.	400,000	Mexican pesos	=	$	
4.	17,500	British pounds	=	$	
5.	30,000	Danish kronen	=	$	

	Converted from American Dollars =	Converted to Foreign Currency	Procedure
6.	$25,000 =	Japanese yen	
7.	$15,000 =	French francs	
8.	$5,000 =	German marks	
9.	$30,000 =	Canadian dollars	
10.	$75,000 =	British pounds	

	Converted from Foreign Currency	=	Converted to Foreign Currency	Procedure
11.	800,000	Japanese yen =	Italian liras	
12.	40,000	German marks =	British pounds	
13.	600,000	Mexican pesos =	French francs	
14.	10,000	So. African rands =	Danish kronen	
15.	15,000	Canadian dollars =	Mexican pesos	

FOREIGN CURRENCY FINANCIAL TRANSACTIONS

A *foreign currency financial transaction* results when a company engages in business with a company from another country, which uses a different currency. For instance, when IBM of the United States buys raw materials from Mexico (which uses the peso) or sells finished products to Germany (which uses the mark), foreign currency financial transactions result.

When companies using different currencies engage in business, they must agree on which country's currency will be used for payment. The currency selected is called the *denominated currency*. For example, if IBM of the United States sells goods to a German company and payment is to be made in marks, the mark is the denominated currency.

Recording Financial Transactions

If, in a transaction between the American company and a foreign company, the American dollar is the denominated currency, the American company will record the transaction in dollars just as if it were a domestic transaction.

If, however, the foreign company's currency is the denominated currency the American company will need to first convert the foreign currency to dollars and then record the transaction in dollars. The exchange rate used is the rate that exists on the date of the transaction. The following two examples help clarify these procedures.

Example 1: American Dollar as Denominated Currency

On June 15, an American company sold goods on account to a French company for $100,000 (American dollars). The American dollar is the denominated currency. Payment is to be made on July 15. On June 15, the direct quote of the French franc is .19337 and the indirect quote is 5.1715. On July 15, the direct quote of the French franc is .18824 and the indirect quote is 5.3125. Present the American company's journal entries to record the June 15 sale and the July 15 receipt of payment.

Solution: (A) Record the June 15 sale on account.

June 15	Accounts Receivable	100,000	
	Sales		100,000

(B) Record the July 15 receipt of payment.

July 15	Cash	100,000	
	Accounts Receivable		100,000

Example 2: Foreign Currency as Denominated Currency

On June 20, an American company purchased goods from a Japanese company for 615,000 yen, submitting payment with the order. Yen is the denominated currency. On June 20, the direct quote of yen is .008078 and the indirect quote is 123.80. Present the American company's journal entry to record the purchase.

Solution: (A) Convert the yen to dollars using the direct quote.
615,000 × .008078 = $4,967.97

(B) Record the June 20 purchase in terms of American dollars.

| June 20 | Purchases | 4,967.97 | |
| | Cash | | 4,967.97 |

As you can see, since the denominated currency is the foreign currency, Japanese yen, the American company converts yen to American dollars and records the transaction in dollars.

Deferred Foreign Currency Transactions

Often, purchases and sales between an American company and a foreign company are credit transactions, calling for payment at a later date. As shown in the preceding example, if the denominated currency is other than the American dollar, an American company converts the foreign currency to dollars before recording the purchase or sale. The currency exchange rate used is the one that exists on the date the purchase, sale, or payment takes place.

If the currency exchange rate changes from the transaction date to the payment date, one of the companies will experience a gain or loss because of the change in value between the foreign currency and the American dollar. The company that will experience the exchange gain or loss is the one that must make or receive payment in a currency other than its own.

For example, suppose an American company buys goods on credit from a German company and the German mark is the denominated currency. When the American company makes payment, it must pay the number of marks specified in the contract. If the value of the mark has increased, it will now take more American dollars to buy the specified number of marks and the American company will recognize a foreign exchange loss. On the other hand, if the value of the mark has decreased, it will take fewer American dollars to buy the specified number of marks and the American company will recognize a foreign exchange gain.

The German company will experience neither a gain nor a loss in either situation since it will receive the number of marks specified in the contract.

The procedures for calculating and recording foreign exchange gains and losses on an American company's records are shown in the following examples.

Example 1: Denominated Currency: American Dollar.
No Foreign Exchange Gain or Loss.

On July 10, an American company sold goods on account to a Mexican company, Gomez, Inc., for $50,000 (American dollars). The American dollar is the denominated currency. Payment is to be made on August 10. On July 10, the direct quote of Mexican pesos is .3259 and the indirect quote is 3.068. On August 10, the direct quote of Mexican pesos is .3207 and the indirect quote is 3.117. Present the American company's journal entries to record the July 10 sale and the August 10 receipt of payment.

Solution: (A) Record the July 10 sale on account.
July 10
Accounts Receivable--Gomez, Inc. 50,000
    Sales   50,000

(B) Record the August 10 receipt of payment.
August 10
Cash   50,000
    Accounts Receivable--Gomez, Inc. 50,000

Since the American dollar is the denominated currency, the American company recorded the sale and receipt of payment in the number of dollars stated and no foreign exchange gain or loss resulted for the American company. However, since the value of the peso dropped from July 10 to August 10, the Mexican company will have an exchange loss, since it will take more pesos to buy the 50,000 American dollars.

Example 2: Denominated Currency: Japanese Yen.
Foreign Exchange Loss.

On July 11, an American company purchased goods on account from a Japanese company, Harima, Inc., for 496,200 yen. The Japa-

nese yen is the denominated currency. Payment is to be made on
August 11. On July 11, the direct quote of yen is .008012 and the
indirect quote is 124.82. On August 11, the direct quote of yen is
.008147 and the indirect quote is 122.75. Present the American company's journal entries to record the July 11 purchase and the August 11
payment.

Solution: Since Japanese yen is the denominated currency, the American company must convert yen to dollars and record the
transactions in terms of dollars. The calculations are as
follows:

(A) July 11 - Convert yen to dollars, using the direct-
quote, to record the purchase on account.
496,200   ×   .008012   = $3,975.55

(B) August 11 - Convert yen to dollars, using the direct
quote, to record the payment.
496,200   ×   .008147   = $4,042.54

(C) August 11 - Calculate the foreign exchange loss.
$4,042.54   − $3,975.55   = $66.99

(D) Record the July 11 purchase on account in terms of
American dollars.
July 11
Purchases   3,975.55
    Accounts Payable--Harima, Inc.   3,975.55

(E) Record the August 11 payment in terms of Ameri-
can dollars, recognizing the foreign exchange loss.
August 11
Accounts Payable--Harima, Inc.   3,975.55
Foreign Exchange Loss   66.99
    Cash   4,042.54

Since the value of Japanese yen increased from the July 11 purchase to the August 11 payment, it will take more American dollars
to buy the 496,200 yen and a foreign exchange loss results for the
American company.

Example 3: Denominated Currency: British Pound.
Foreign Exchange Gain.

On July 12, an American company purchased goods on account from a British company, Londonaire, Inc., for 3,924 British pounds. The British pound is the denominated currency. Payment is to be made August 12. On July 12, the direct quote for British pounds is 1.5325 and the indirect quote is .6525. On August 12, the direct quote for British pounds is 1.5145 and the indirect quote is .6603. Present the American company's journal entries to record the July 12 purchase and the August 12 payment.

Solution: Since the British pound is the denominated currency, the American company must convert pounds to dollars and record the transactions in terms of dollars. The calculations are as follows:

(A) July 12 - Convert pounds to dollars, using the direct quote, to record the purchase.
3,924 $\times$ 1.5325 = $6,013.53

(B) August 12 - Convert pounds to dollars, using the direct quote, to record the payment.
3,924 $\times$ 1.5145 = $5,942.90

(C) August 12 - Calculate the foreign exchange gain.
$6,013.53 − $5,942.90 = $70.63

(D) Record the July 12 purchase on account in terms of American dollars.
July 12
Purchases   6,013.53
   Accounts Payable--Londonaire, Inc.   6,013.53

(E) Record the August 11 payment in terms of American dollars, recognizing the foreign exchange gain.
August 12
Accounts Payable--Londonaire, Inc.   6,013.53
   Foreign Exchange Gain   70.63
   Cash   5,942.90

Since the value of the British pound decreased from the July 12 purchase to the August 12 payment, it will take fewer American dollars to buy the 3,924 British pounds and a foreign exchange gain results for the American company.

Practice Problems: Deferred Foreign Currency Transactions

Record the transactions listed below. Use the Monday prices from the July 15 currency exchange rate quotations and the Thursday prices from the August 15 currency exchange rate quotations. Present your calculations in good order in the blank space following each question.

After you have completed your work, refer to the answers at the back of this training manual to check your answers and to verify your procedures.

CURRENCY EXCHANGE RATES
July 15
(Use Monday's Prices)

	Foreign Currency In Dollars (Direct Quote)		Dollar in Foreign Currency (Indirect Quote)	
	Mon.	Tue.	Mon.	Tue.
Austria	.0899	.0899	11.121	11.128
Italy	.000713	.000712	1402.00	1404.00
Spain	.008857	.008853	112.90	112.95

CURRENCY EXCHANGE RATES
August 15
(Use Thursday's Prices)

	Foreign Currency In Dollars (Direct Quote)		Dollar in Foreign Currency (Indirect Quote)	
	Thur.	Wed.	Thur.	Wed.
Austria	.09563	.09583	10.460	10.430
Italy	.0007619	.0007656	1312.59	1306.10
Spain	.008578	.008708	116.57	114.84

1. On July 15, an American company sold goods on account to an Austrian company, Starr, Inc., for $25,000 (American dollars). The American dollar is the denominated currency. Payment was made on August 15. Record (A) the sale on July 15 and (B) the receipt of payment on August 15.

Present your calculations below:

Record journal entries on following page.

Date	Description	Post. Ref.	Debit	Credit

Journal   Page

42

2. On July 15, an American company purchased goods on account from an Italian company, Minelli, Inc., for 4,206,000 liras. The Italian lira is the denominated currency. Payment was made on August 15. Record (A) the purchase on July 15 and (B) the payment on August 15.

Present your calculations below:

Record journal entries on following page.

Date	Description	Post. Ref.	Debit	Credit

Journal   Page

3. On July 15, an American company purchased goods on account from a Spanish company, Merida, Inc., for 564,500 pesetas. The Spanish peseta is the denominated currency. Payment was made on August 15. Record (A) the purchase on July 15, and (B) the payment on August 15.

Present your calculations below:

Record journal entries on following page.

Journal				Page	
Date	Description	Post. Ref.	Debit		Credit

46

Foreign Currency Transactions Adjustment

At the end of an accounting period when financial statements are prepared, there may be unsettled foreign currency transactions. For instance, an American company may prepare its quarterly financial statements on March 31. A purchase on account from a foreign company on March 25, calling for payment on April 25, will be unsettled on the March 31 financial statement date.

If the foreign currency is the denominated currency, and the currency exchange rate has fluctuated from the transaction date, an adjusting entry is required. The exchange gain or loss from the transaction date to the financial statement date is recorded. As you will see, the procedure is identical to that used in calculating and recording foreign exchange gains and losses on deferred foreign currency transactions, as described in the preceding section.

Example 1: Denominated Currency: Swiss franc.
Adjustment for Foreign Currency Loss.

On March 25, an American company purchased goods on account from a Swiss company, Matterhorn Outfitters, for 8,000 Swiss francs. Payment is to be made April 25. The Swiss franc is the denominated currency. The American company's financial period ends March 31. On March 25, the direct quote for the Swiss franc is .6739 and the indirect quote is 1.4840. On March 31, the direct quote for the Swiss franc is .6892 and the indirect quote 1.4510. Present the American company's March 31 adjusting entry to record the foreign exchange gain or loss.

Solution: Since the Swiss franc is the denominated currency, the American company must convert francs to dollars to record the purchase and the adjusting entry. The calculations are as follows:

(A) March 25 - Convert francs to dollars, using the direct quote, to record purchase on account.
8,000 $\times$ .6739 = $5,391.20

(B) For reference purposes, show the entry made to record the March 25 purchase.

March 25
Purchases	5,391.20	
Accts. Pay.--Matterhorn Outfitters		5,391.20

(C) March 31 - Convert francs to dollars to determine amount owed on financial statement date, using the direct quote.

$$8,000 \ \times \ .6892 \ = \ \$5,513.60$$

(D) Compute the foreign exchange gain or loss.

$$\$5,513.60 \ - \ \$5,391.20 \ = \ \$122.40 \text{ loss}$$

(E) Record the March 31 adjusting entry.

March 31
Foreign Exchange Loss	122.40	
Accts. Pay.--Matterhorn Outfitters		122.40

Example 2: Denominated Currency: Italian lira.
Adjustment for Foreign Currency Gain.

On March 20, an American company sold goods on account to an Italian company, Treviso, Inc., with payment to be made on April 20. The Italian lira is the denominated currency. At the end of the accounting period, March 31, there is a foreign exchange gain of $128.60. Present the adjusting entry to recognize this exchange gain.

Solution: March 31
Accounts Receivable--Treviso, Inc.	128.60	
Foreign Exchange Gain		128.60

Practice Problems: Foreign Currency Transactions Adjustment

Calculate the adjustment amount and prepare the adjusting entries for each of the following transactions. The accounting period ends March 31. Present your calculations in good order in the blank space following each question.

After you have completed your work, refer to the answers at the back of this training manual to check your answers and to verify your procedures.

1. On March 10, an American company purchased goods on account from a Portuguese company, Setubal, Inc., for 300,000 Portuguese escudos, with payment to be made on April 10. The escudo is the denominated currency. On March 10, the direct quote for the escudo was .007450 and the indirect quote was 134.23. On March 31, the direct quote for the escudo was .007551 and the indirect quote was 132.44.

Present your calculations below:

Record journal entries on following page.

Date	Description	Post. Ref.	Debit	Credit

Journal

Page

2. On March 11, an American company sold goods on account to an Irish company, Edenderry, Inc., for 2,000 Irish punt, with payment to be made on April 11. The punt is the denominated currency. On March 11, the direct quote for Irish punt was 1.6757 and the indirect quote was .5968. On March 31, the direct quote for Irish punt was 1.6282 and the indirect quote was .6142.

Present your calculations below:

Record journal entries on following page.

Journal

Page ___

Date	Description	Post. Ref.	Debit	Credit

3. On March 12, an American company purchased goods on account from an Indian company, Bombay Trading Co., for 65,000 Indian rupees, with payment to be made on April 12. The Indian rupee is the denominated currency. On March 12, the direct quote for the Indian rupee was .03876 and the indirect quote was 25.80. On March 31, the direct quote for the rupee was .03820 and the indirect quote was 26.18.

Present your calculations below:

Record journal entries on following page.

Journal

Page

Date	Description	Post. Ref.	Debit	Credit

54

FOREIGN CURRENCY
FINANCIAL STATEMENTS

Often, when an American company has a subsidiary that operates in a foreign country, the foreign subsidiary will record all of its own day-to-day transactions and prepare its own financial statements. Periodically, this information is transferred to the American company's accounting department. For instance, sales information may be transferred on a daily basis. Other information, like financial statements, may be submitted monthly or quarterly.

Usually, a foreign subsidiary will record its financial transactions and financial data in its own country's currency. In order for the American company to utilize this financial information, amounts are converted to American dollars using an accounting process called *translation*.

Some foreign subsidiaries record all financial transactions in American dollars as they occur. Thus, no translation is required since the amounts are already in American dollars.

In a few rare instances, when a foreign subsidiary is located in a country with a high rate of inflation or highly unstable currency, the financial transactions may be recorded in a different foreign country's currency, which is more stable. Before this financial information can be utilized by the American company, an accounting process called *remeasurement* is used. After remeasurement, the accounting records will reflect the same results as if the transaction had been recorded in American dollars in the first place.

The accounting term, *functional currency*, is used to identify the most logical and appropriate currency for a foreign subsidiary to select, based on the currency it uses most for cash payments and receipts. Once the functional currency is identified, the accountant will know which conversion process to use–translation or remeasurement. Since most foreign subsidiaries' functional currency is their own country's currency and since they also record their transactions in the same currency, translation is the process that is used most often.

At the Karissa Jean's Paris subsidiary, the French franc is used for cash receipts and payments. Therefore, the French franc is the functional currency. All transactions and financial data are also recorded in the French franc. Therefore, the accounting process of translation is used to convert the Paris subsidiary data from French francs to American dollars.

Translation

At the end of each accounting period (monthly, quarterly, annually, etc.) the foreign subsidiary's balance sheet and income statement amounts are converted from the foreign currency to American dollars using the accounting process of translation. There are several FASB-52 guidelines that must be followed:

1. When translating asset and liability amounts, use the currency exchange rate that exists on the balance sheet date, called the *current rate.*
2. When translating capital stock amounts, use the currency exchange rate that existed on the date the foreign subsidiary was established or purchased, called the *historical rate.*
3. When translating dividend amounts, use the currency exchange rate on the date of declaration.
4. When translating income statement items, use the weighted-average exchange rate. The *weighted-average* for a particular time period is computed by adding the currency exchange rate quotes and dividing by the number of days in that time period. Since computing the weighted-average for a lengthy period, such as a year, is a laborious task, most international accounting departments obtain the weighted-average from a financial service or publication such as the *The Wall Street Journal.*
5. Recall that the retained earnings for the balance sheet is computed by adding net income and subtracting dividends from the beginning retained earnings. Since the net income and dividend amounts have already been translated, no further translation is required.
6. Since three different rates, the current exchange rate, the historical rate, and the weighted-average rate, are used in translating balance sheet and income statement amounts, debits and credits will no longer be equal after translation. Therefore, the difference between debits and credits, called the *translation adjustment*, is reported in the stockholder's equity section of the balance sheet.

Example: Financial Statement Translation

Abbreviated forms of the income statement, retained earnings statement, and balance sheet for French Company, Inc. are shown below. Following the financial statements is the currency exchange rate information needed to do translation. The solution below shows how the financial statements were translated from French francs to American dollars. Translated amounts are rounded to the nearest dollar.

French Company, Inc.
Income Statement (in Francs)
Month Ending June 30, 19--

	(In Francs)
Sales	152,000
Cost of Goods Sold	85,000
Gross Profit	67,000
Expenses	27,000
Net Income	40,000

French Company, Inc.
Retained Earnings Statement (in Francs)
Month Ending June 30, 19--

	(In Francs)
Retained Earnings, June 1, 19--	35,000
Add: Net Income	40,000
Less: Dividends	10,000
Retained Earnings, June 30, 19--	65,000

French Company, Inc.
Balance Sheet (in Francs)
June 30, 19--

Assets	(In Francs)
Cash	20,000
Accounts Receivable	25,000
Merchandise Inventory	50,000
Equipment (Book Value)	80,000
Total Assets	175,000

Liabilities	
Accounts Payable	22,000
Notes Payable	63,000
Total Liabilities	85,000

Stockholder's Equity	
Common Stock	25,000
Retained Earnings	65,000
Total Stockholder's Equity	90,000
Total Liabilities & Stockholder's Equity	175,000

Translation Information

The following currency exchange rates are used in making the financial statement translations. Also shown is May's ending translated retained earnings amount (shown in dollars), which will be used as June's beginning retained earnings amount on the translated retained earnings statement.

The information was obtained from financial publications and from French Company's records.

Currency Exchange Rates (Direct Quote of French Franc)

Current Rate, June 30	.18104
Weighted-Average for Month of June	.18172
Rate on Dividend Declaration Date	.18065
Rate on Date Subsidiary Established	.17095
Beginning Translated Retained Earnings	$6,238 (in Dollars)

Solution: Translated Income Statement

To translate the income statement from French francs to American Dollars, multiply each amount by the weighted average for the month of June. (Translated amounts are rounded to the nearest dollar.)

French Company, Inc.
Income Statement (in Dollars)
Month Ending June 30, 19--   (Procedure)

Sales	$27,621	(152,000 francs × .18172)
Cost of Goods Sold	15,446	(85,000 francs × .18172)
Gross Profit	$12,175	(Sales – Cost of Goods Sold)
Expenses	4,906	(27,000 francs × .18172)
Net Income	$7,269	(Gross Profit – Expenses)

Solution: Translated Retained Earnings Statement

— June's beginning retained earnings amount is the ending retained earnings from May's translated retained earnings statement and is already shown in dollars.

- The net income amount is taken from the June translated income statement (shown above) and is already stated in dollars.
- The dividend amount shown on the retained earnings statement is translated from francs to dollars by multiplying by the currency exchange rate on the date the dividend was declared.

French Company, Inc. Retained Earnings Statement (in Dollars) Month Ending June 30, 19--	(Procedure)
Retained Earnings, June 1 .. $ 6,238	(From Translation Information)
Add: Net Income for June 7,269	(From June Income Statement)
Less: Dividends 1,807	(10,000 francs x .18065)
Retained Earnings, June 30 $11,700	(Beg. R.E. + N.I. - Dividends)

Solution: Translated Balance Sheet

- Asset and liability amounts are translated from francs to dollars using the currency exchange rate on the balance sheet date.
- The capital stock amount is translated from francs to dollars by using the currency exchange rate that existed on the date the subsidiary was established, which is found in the company's records (the historical rate).
- The retained earnings amount is taken from the translated retained earnings statement for the month ending June 30 (shown above), and is already stated in dollars.
- Because translations on the income statement, retained earnings statement, and balance sheet used different exchange rates (current, weighted-average, historical), debits and credits are no longer equal. Therefore, a translation adjustment is required.

Total assets must equal total liabilities plus stockholder's equity. Before translation adjustment, assets equal $31,682 and liabilities plus stockholder's equity equal $31,363. Therefore, $319 ($31,682 − $31,363 = $319) must be added as a translation adjustment to balance the balance sheet. (Note: If stockholder's equity plus liabilities had exceeded total assets, the difference would have been subtracted as a translation adjustment.)

French Company, Inc.
Balance Sheet (in Dollars)
June 30, 19--

Assets		(Procedure)
Cash	$3,621	(20,000 francs × .18104)
Accounts Receivable	4,526	(25,000 francs × .18104)
Merchandise Inventory	9,052	(50,000 francs × .18104)
Equipment (Book Value)	14,483	(80,000 francs × .18104)
Total Assets	$31,682	(Total of Asset Amounts)
Liabilities		
Accounts Payable	$ 3,983	(22,000 francs × .18104)
Notes Payable	11,406	(63,000 francs × .18104)
Total Liabilities	$15,389	(Total of Liability Amounts)
Stockholder's Equity		
Common Stock	$ 4,274	(25,000 francs × .17095)
Retained Earnings	11,700	(From June 30 R.E. Statement)
Add: Trans.Adjustment	319	(To balance Balance Sheet)
Total Stk. Equity	$16,293	(Total Stockholder Equity Amounts)
Total Liabilities and		
Stockholder's Equity	$31,682	(After Translation Adjustment, Assets = Liab. + Stockholder Equity)

Practice Problems: Financial Statement Translation

Abbreviated forms of the income statement, retained earnings statement, and balance sheet for Lussier Company, a French corporation, are shown below. Using the exchange rates provided, prepare the translated income statement, retained earnings statement, and balance sheet for Lussier Company.

Round translated amounts to the nearest dollar. After you have completed your work, refer to the answers at the back of this training manual to check your answers.

Translation Information–Currency Exchange Rates (Direct Quote of French Franc)

Current Rate, September 30	.18191
Weighted-Average for Month of September	.18005
Rate on Dividend Declaration Date	.18243
Rate on Date Subsidiary Established	.17189
Beginning Translated Retained Earnings	$301,589 (in $)

Lussier Company
Income Statement (in Francs)
Month Ending September 30, 19--

	(in Francs)
Sales	458,580
Cost of Goods Sold	197,190
Gross Profit	261,390
Expenses	160,503
Net Income	100,887

Lussier Company
Retained Earnings Statement (in Francs)
Month Ending September 30, 19--

	(in Francs)
Retained Earnings, September 1, 19--	1,675,492
Add Net Income for September	100,887
Less Dividends	27,483
Retained Earnings, September 30, 19--	1,748,896

Lussier Company
Balance Sheet (in Francs)
September 30, 19--

Assets	(in Francs)
Cash	943,127
Other Assets	3,872,391
Total Assets	4,815,518

Liabilities	
Accounts Payable	837,218
Other Liabilities	1,729,404
Total Liabilities	2,566,622

Stockholder's Equity	
Common Stock	500,000
Retained Earnings	1,748,896
Total Stockholder's Equity	2,248,896
Total Liabilities & Stockholder's Equity	4,815,518

Present your translated Income Statement and Retained Earnings Statement for Lussier Company below in rough draft. Show your calculations in the margin.

Present your translated Balance Sheet for Lussier Company below in rough draft. Show your calculations in the margin.

Chapter 6

More About Karissa Jean's

Now that you have a basic understanding of international business and international accounting, it is time to learn the rest of the story about Karissa Jean's.

In 1991, Karissa Jean's purchased the office and warehouse space in Denver that had been leased since 1987. And, as previously mentioned, the decision was made to begin marketing Karissa Jean's jeans internationally.

After much research, it was decided that Japan and Great Britain would be ideal countries in which to sell Karissa Jean's jeans. After studying all of the methods available for selling jeans in those two countries, it was decided that exporting would be the ideal method.

With the help of the United States Department of Commerce and the Colorado International Trade Authority, several garment distributors were identified in each country that were eager to import American-made jeans. Karissa and sales manager, Sean McMasters, traveled to each country and interviewed all prospective distributors. In March 1991, agreements were made with Hasaki Corporation of Tokyo, Japan, and Wellington, Ltd., of London, England, for distribution of Karissa Jean's jeans. Exporting to these two countries began in May 1991. The jeans were an immediate success in each country.

In December 1991, with great regret, Wellington, Ltd. asked that it be allowed to terminate its distribution agreement with Karissa Jean's. This became necessary because of a conflict of interest clause in a contract between Wellington and one of its long-time business associates. This was a mixed blessing for Karissa Jean's. Although Wellington had done an outstanding job, termination of the distribution agreement allowed Karissa Jean's to pursue other, more lucrative, distribution plans.

In February 1992, Karissa Jean's established its own marketing subsidiary in Paris, France, called Karissa Jean's France, to distribute Karissa Jean's jeans itself to the 12 countries in the European Community. Sean McMasters was appointed manager of Karissa Jean's France, which now employs 12 office personnel, eight warehouse workers, and ten salespeople. In June 1992, arrangements were made with a Paris garment manufacturer, M'Sharee, to manufacture jeans on a contract basis, using Karissa Jean's designs and patterns. Karissa Jeans's France markets these jeans throughout the European Community.

Recently, Karissa Jean's has begun exporting jeans to Canada and Australia from the Denver home office. Exporting of jeans to Japan continues at a lively pace. Karissa Jean's is currently exploring the sale of its jeans to other countries and is exploring the possibility of adding shirts and blouses to its clothing line.

And, now, you know how Karissa Jean Fowler started Karissa Jean's, why the company is called Karissa Jean's, and why Karissa Jean's jeans are called Karissa Jean's jeans!

COMPLETING KARISSA JEAN'S TRAINING PROGRAM

Most likely, you are anxious to get started with your duties in Karissa Jean's International Accounting Department. But, first, you must complete Karissa Jean's training program. Complete Progress Test 3 and then follow your immediate supervisor's instructions for taking the Training Exam, which covers all of the material in this training manual, before reporting to work in the international accounting department.

PROGRESS TEST 3

This self-test is presented to allow you to measure your comprehension of the material presented in the *International Accounting* and *More About Karissa Jean's* sections of this training manual. After you have completed this self-test, compare your answers to those found in the back of this manual. Use the following grading scale to evaluate your comprehension of this material and to determine what to do next.

Points Correct	*Evaluation*
14-15	*Excellent!* You have studied this section of the training manual thoroughly. You are well prepared to perform your international accounting duties.
12-13	*Good!* You have a good command of the information presented. You should, however, quickly review the areas you missed.
10-11	*Fair.* A more serious effort is required on your part. Thoroughly review the section on international accounting before you proceed.
Below 10	*Poor.* You *must* devote more time and effort to studying this training manual or you will be incompetent to perform your duties at Karissa Jean's. Go back and study the international accounting section from the beginning before you proceed.

1. The direct quote for the Netherlands guilder is .5426 and the indirect quote is 1.8429. How many Netherlands guilders can 200,000 American dollars be converted to?

2. The direct quote for the Saudi Arabian riyal is .26665 and the indirect quote is 3.7503. How many American dollars can 7,500 Saudi Arabian riyals be converted to?

3. The direct quote of the Canadian dollar is .8753 and the indirect quote is 1.1425. The direct quote of the Greek drachma is .005714 and the indirect quote is 175.02. How many Greek drachmas can 20,000 Canadian dollars be converted to?

4. On August 10, an American company sold goods to an Austrian company, Alpbach, Inc., on account for $30,000 (American dollars). The American dollar is the denominated currency. Payment is to be made on September 10. On August 10, the direct quote of the Austrian schilling is .09372 and the indirect quote is 10.67. On September 10, the direct quote of the Austrian schilling is .09013 and the indirect quote is 11.09. Present the American company's journal entries to record the August 10 sale and the September 10 receipt of payment.

Date	Description	Post. Ref.	Debit	Credit

Journal   Page

5. On August 11, an American company purchased goods from a Spanish company, Madridejos Company, for 80,000 Spanish pesetas, submitting payment with the order. The peseta is the denominated currency. On August 11, the direct quote of the Spanish peseta was .010403 and the indirect quote was 96.13. Present the American company's journal entry to record the August 11 purchase.

Journal

Page

Date	Description	Post. Ref.	Debit	Credit

6. On August 12, an American company purchased goods on account from a Venezuelan company, Calabozo, Inc., for 148,000 Venezuelan bolivars. The bolivar is the denominated currency. Payment is to be made on September 12. On August 12, the direct quote of the Venezuelan bolivar is .01301 and the indirect quote is 76.88. On September 12, the direct quote of Venezuelan bolivar is .01548 and the indirect quote is 64.62. Present the American company's journal entries to record the August 12 purchase and the September 12 payment.

Journal

Page

Date	Description	Post. Ref.	Debit	Credit

7. On August 14, an American company purchased goods on account from a Portuguese company, Monsaraz, Inc., for 150,000 Portuguese escudos. The Portuguese escudo is the denominated currency. Payment is to be made September 14. On August 14, the direct quote of escudos is .007913 and the indirect quote is 126.37. On September 14, the direct quote of escudos is .007576 and the indirect quote is 131.99. Present the American company's journal entries to record the August 14 purchase and the September 14 payment.

Journal

Page ____

Date	Description	Post. Ref.	Debit	Credit

8. On June 15, an American company purchased goods on account from a Canadian company, Scarborough, Inc., for 4,000 Canadian dollars, with payment to be made on July 15. The Canadian dollar is the denominated currency. The American company's accounting period ends June 30. On June 15, the direct quote for the Canadian dollar was .8367 and the indirect quote was 1.1952. On June 30, the direct quote of the Canadian dollar was .8410 and the indirect quote was 1.1891. Present the American company's June 30 adjusting entry to record the foreign exchange gain or loss.

Journal

Page ___

Date	Description	Post. Ref.	Debit	Credit

9. On June 16, an American company purchased goods on account from an Italian company, Mazzini, Inc., for 250,000 Italian liras, with payment to be made on July 16. The Italian lira is the denominated currency. The American company's accounting period ends June 30. On June 16, the direct quote for the Italian lira was .0008140 and the indirect quote was 1228.44. On June 30, the direct quote for the Italian lira was .0008034 and the indirect quote was 1244.70. Present the American company's June 30 adjusting entry to record the foreign exchange gain or loss.

Journal

Page

Date	Description	Post. Ref.	Debit	Credit

10. When translating a foreign subsidiary's asset and liability amounts on the balance sheet to American dollars, the _____ currency exchange rate should be used. (A) Current (B) Historical (C) Weighted Average (D) Translated

11. When translating foreign subsidiary income statement items to American dollars, use the _____ currency exchange rate. (A) Current (B) Historical (C) Weighted-Average (D) Translated

12. When translating foreign subsidiary capital stock amounts to American dollars, use the _____ currency exchange rate. (A) Current (B) Historical (C) Weighted-Average (D) Translated

13. Since the debits and credits on the translated balance sheet will no longer be equal because various translation rates have been used, a _____ is reported in the stockholder's equity section of the balance sheet to make it balance. (A) Net Income or Net Loss (B) Stock Dividend (C) Translation Adjustment (D) Translated Remeasurement

14. To what three countries does Karissa Jean's export to from its Denver, Colorado, office? (A) France, Denmark, Germany (B) Japan, France, Austria (C) Canada, Mexico, Japan (D) Canada, Japan, Australia

15. In what city is Karissa Jean's marketing subsidiary located? (A) Tokyo, Japan (B) Montreal, Canada (C) Paris, France (D) Mexico City, Mexico

TRAINING EXAM

You have now completed the training manual at Karissa Jean's. The next step is to take a *Training Exam* to measure your comprehension of this material.

Since it is extremely important that you demonstrate a full command of the international business and accounting principles presented in this training manual, it is suggested that you review before taking the training exam.

After you have completed the training exam, report to your supervisor, Beverly Carter, in the International Accounting Department to begin your duties at Karissa Jean's.

ANSWERS TO TRAINING MANUAL PROGRESS TESTS AND PRACTICE PROBLEMS

Use these answers to check the accuracy of your work and to verify your procedures. If any of your answers are incorrect, review that section before proceeding.

ANSWERS TO PROGRESS TESTS

Progress Test 1 – Chapter 2, Page 11

1. D
2. B
3. C
4. C
5. C
6. A
7. B
8. B
9. D
10. B
11. A
12. C
13. D
14. B
15. A

Progress Test 2 – Chapter 4, Page 25

1. D
2. B
3. B
4. C
5. A
6. C
7. D
8. C
9. C
10. B
11. D
12. A
13. B
14. C
15. A

Progress Test 3 – Chapter 6, Page 66

1. 368,580 Netherlands guilders   (200,000 × 1.8429 = 368,580)
2. 1,999.88 American dollars   (7,500 × .26665 = $1,999.88)
3. 3,063,900.12 Greek drachmas   (Convert Canadian dollars to American dollars)
20,000 × .8753 = $17,506.00
(Convert American dollars to Greek drachmas)
$17,506.00 × 175.02 = 3,063,900.12

4. August 10

Accounts Receivable—Alpbach, Inc.	30,000	
Sales		30,000

September 10

Cash	30,000	
Accounts Receivable—Alpbach, Inc.		30,000

5. August 11

Purchases	832.24	
Cash		832.24

(80,000 pesetas × .010403 = $832.24)

6. August 12
Purchases   1,925.48
    Accounts Payable—Calabozo, Inc.   1,925.48
    (148,000 bolivars × .01301 = $1,925.48)
September 12
Accounts Payable—Calabozo, Inc.   1,925.48
Foreign Exchange Loss   365.56
    Cash   2,291.04
    (148,000 bolivars × .01548 = $2,291.04)
    ($2,291.04 − $1.925.48 = $365.56 Loss)
7. August 14
Purchases   1,186.95
    Accounts Payable—Monsaraz, Inc.   1,186.95
    (150,000 escudos × .007913 = $1,186.95)
September 14
Accounts Payable—Monsaraz, Inc.   1,186.95
    Foreign Exchange Gain   50.55
    Cash   1,136.40
    (150,000 escudos × .007576 = $1,136.40)
    ($1,186.95 − $1,136.40 = $50.55 Gain)
8. June 30
Foreign Exchange Loss   17.20
    Accounts Payable—Scarborough, Inc.   17.20
    (June 15 Purchase − 4,000 Canadian dollars × .8367 = $3,346.80)
    (June 30 − 4,000 Canadian dollars × .8410 = $3,364.00)
    ($3,364.00 − $3,346.80 = $17.20 Loss)
9. June 30
Accounts Payable—Mazzini, Inc.   2.65
    Foreign Exchange Gain   2.65
    (June 16 Purchase − 250,000 liras × .0008140 = $203.50)
    (June 30 − 250,000 liras × .0008034 = $200.85)
    ($203.50 − $200.85 = $2.65 Gain)
10. A
11. C
12. B

13. C
14. D
15. C

ANSWERS TO PRACTICE PROBLEMS

Currency Exchange Rates – Page 32

	Converted from Foreign Currency	=	Converted to American Dollars	Foreign Currency Amount	×	Direct Quote	=	American Dollars
						Procedure		
1.	15,000 Canadian dollars	=	$11,790.00	15,000	×	.7860	=	$11,790.00
2.	250,000 Japanese yen	=	$2,017.00	250,000	×	.008068	=	$2,017.00
3.	400,000 Mexican pesos	=	$128,400.00	400,000	×	.321	=	$128,400.00
4.	17,500 British pounds	=	$27,921.25	17,500	×	1.5955	=	$27,921.25
5.	30,000 Danish kronen	=	$4,986.00	30,000	×	.1662	=	$4,986.00

	Converted from American Dollars	=	Converted to Foreign Currency		Dollars	×	Indirect Quote	=	Foreign Currency Amount
							Procedure		
6.	$25,000	=	3,098,750.00	Japanese yen	$25,000	×	123.95	=	3,098,750.00
7.	$15,000	=	79,605.00	French francs	$15,000	×	5.3070	=	79,605.00
8.	$5,000	=	7,785.00	German marks	$5,000	×	1.5570	=	7,785.00
9.	$30,000	=	38,166.00	Canadian dollars	$30,000	×	1.2722	=	38,166.00
10.	$75,000	=	47,010.00	British pounds	$75,000	×	.6268	=	47,010.000

	Converted from Foreign Currency	=	Converted to Foreign Currency		Procedure
11.	800,000 Japanese yen	=	8,868,345.60	Italian liras	*Step 1*–Convert yen to dollars 800,000 × .008068 = $6,454.40
					Step 2–Convert dollars to liras $6,454.40 × 1,374 = 8,868,345.60
12.	40,000 German marks	=	16,103.75	British pounds	*Step 1*–Convert marks to dollars 40,000 × .6423 = $25.692.00
					Step 2–Convert dollars to pounds $25,692.00 × .6268 = 16,103.75
13.	600,000 Mexican pesos	=	1,022,128.20	French francs	*Step 1*–Convert pesos to dollars 600,000 × .321 = $192,600.00
					Step 2–Convert dollars to francs $192,600.00 × 5.3070 = 1,022,128.20
14.	10,000 So. African rands	=	20,191.37	Danish kronen	*Step 1*–Convert rands to dollars 10,000 × .3356 = $3,356.00
					Step 2–Convert dollars to kronen $3,356.00 × 6.0165 = 20,191.37
15.	15,000 Canadian dollars	=	36,725.85	Mexi- can pesos	*Step 1*–Convert Canadian dollars to American dollars 15,000 × .7860 = $11,790.00
					Step 2–Convert American dollars to pesos $11,790.00 × 3.115 = 36,725.85

Deferred Foreign Currency Transactions – Page 40

1. July 15
   Accounts Receivable—Starr, Inc.   25,000.00
       Sales   25,000.00
   August 15
   Cash   25,000.00
       Accounts Receivable—Starr, Inc.   25,000.00
       (Since the American dollar is the denominated currency,
       the American company records the transaction in the
       number of dollars involved in the transaction.)

2. July 15
   Purchases   2,998.88
       Accounts Payable—Minelli, Inc.   2,998.88
       (4,206,000 lira × .000713 = $2,998.88)
   August 15
   Accounts Payable—Minelli, Inc.   2,998.88
   Foreign Exchange Loss   205.67
       Cash   3,204.55
       (4,206,000 liras × .0007619 = $3,204.55)
       ($3,204.55 – $2,998.88 = $205.67 Loss)

3. July 15
   Purchases   4,999.78
       Accounts Payable—Merida, Inc.   4,999.78
       (564,500 pesetas × .008857 = $4,999.78)
   August 15
   Accounts Payable—Merida, Inc.   4,999.78
       Foreign Exchange Gain   157.50
       Cash   4,842.28
       (564,500 pesetas × .008578 = $4,842.28)
       ($4,999.78 – $4,842.28 = $157.50 Gain)

Foreign Currency Transactions Adjustment – Page 48

1. March 31
   Foreign Exchange Loss   30.30
       Accounts Payable—Setubal, Inc.   30.30
       (March 10 – Purchase: 300,000 escudos × .007450 =
       $2,235.00)

(March 31 – Accounts Payable: 300,000 escudos ×
.007551 = $2,265.30)
(March 31 – Adjustment: $2,265.30 – $2,235.00 =
$30.30 Loss)

2. March 31
Foreign Exchange Loss 95.00
    Accounts Receivable—Edenderry, Inc. 95.00
(March 11 – Sale: 2,000 punt × 1.6757 = $3,351.40)
(March 31 – Accounts Receivable: 2,000 punt ×
1.6282 = $3,256.40)
(March 31 – Adjustment: $3,351.40 – $3,256.40 =
$95.00 Loss)

3. March 31
Accounts Payable—Bombay Trading Co. 36.40
    Foreign Currency Gain 36.40
(March 12 – Purchase: 65,000 rupees × .03876 =
$2,519.40)
(March 31 – Accounts Payable: 65,000 rupees ×
.03820 = $2,483.00)
(March 31 – Adjustment: $2,519.40 – $2,483.00 =
$36.40 Gain)

Financial Statement Translation – Page 60

Lussier Company
Income Statement (in Dollars)
Month Ending September 30, 19—

		(Procedure)
Sales	$82,567	(458,580 francs × .18005)
Cost of Goods Sold	35,504	(197,190 francs × .18005)
Gross Profit	$47,063	(Sales – Cost of Goods Sold)
Expenses	28,899	(160,503 francs × .18005)
Net Income	$18,164	(Gross Profit – Expenses)

Lussier Company
Retained Earnings Statement (in Dollars)
Month Ending September 30, 19—

		(Procedure)
Retained Earnings, September 1	$301,589	(From Translation Information)
Add: Net Income for September	18,164	(From 9-30 Income Statement)
Less: Dividends	5,014	(27,483 francs x .18243)
Retained Earnings, September 30	$314,739	(9–1 R.E. + N.I. – Dividends)

Lussier Company
Balance Sheet (in Dollars)
September 30, 19—

Assets   (Procedure)

		(Procedure)
Assets		
Cash	$171,564	(943,127 francs × .18191)
Other Assets	704,427	(3,872,391 francs × .18191)
Total Assets	$875,991	(Total of Asset Amounts)
Liabilities		
Accounts Payable	$152,298	(837,218 francs × .18191)
Other Liabilities	314,596	(1,729,404 francs × .18191)
Total Liabilities	$466,894	(Total of Liability Amounts)
Stockholder's Equity		
Common Stock	$ 85,945	(500,000 francs × .17189)
Retained Earnings	314,739	(From 9–30 R.E. Statement)
Add: Translation Adjustment	8,413	(To balance Balance Sheet)
Total Stockholder's Equity	$409,097	(Total of Stk. Equity Amounts)
Total Liabilities and		
Stockholder's Equity	$875,991	(After Translation Adjustment, Assets = Liab. + Stk. Equity)

Karissa Jean's®

International Accounting Department

(Simulation)

Inter-Office Memo

Karissa Jean's®

To: International Accountant

From: Beverly Carter,
International Accounting
Department Manager

Subject: Starting Your International Accounting Duties

Date: January 18, 19—

Congratulations on completing Karissa Jean's International Accounting Training Program. I'm sure you will find that it has properly prepared you to perform all of your duties in the International Accounting Department.

All of your duties and assignments will be relayed to you via memos and other written communications (our standard policy—so there is no error in verbal interpretation). Feel free to refer to your Training Manual for guidance; or, ask if you have any questions.

All of us in the International Accounting Department are looking forward to working with you.

Inter-Office Memo

Karissa Jean's®

To: International Accountant

From: Bev Carter

Subject: Estimate of Funds Needed for Trip Abroad

Date: January 18, 19—

Karissa is considering a business trip to Ireland, Portugal, Spain, Italy, and France. As you will see from the attached letter from our travel agent, the agent estimated the cost of the trip in terms of each country's currency.

Please convert each of these amounts to American dollars so Karissa can see what the approximate cost will be. Please list the amounts on the lines I've drawn on the travel agent's letter. You can use the currency exchange rates below. Thanks.

Currency	Direct Quote	Indirect Quote
Irish punt	1.6946	.5901
Portuguese escudo	.007177	139.33
Spanish peseta	.009006	111.04
Italian lira	.0007118	1404.99
French franc	.18771	5.3275

WORld-WIde Travel Agency, Inc.
3610 Chambers
Aurora, CO 80245

January 15, 19--

Ms. Karissa Fowler
KARISSA JEAN'S
8677 Colfax Avenue
Denver, CO 80227

Dear Ms. Fowler:

This is to confirm our earlier telephone conversation about
your inquiry for the following flight itinerary: Denver -
Dublin, Ireland - Lisbon, Portugal - Madrid, Spain - Naples,
Italy - Paris, France - Denver. The first-class flight is
$3,149. Other costs you inquired about are estimated below:

CONVERTED TO AMERICAN $

Dublin, Ireland
Lodging - 2 nights   205 punt
Food - 3 days   70 punt
Ground transportation   30 punt
                             TOTAL:

Lisbon, Portugal
Lodging - 1 night   25,000 escudos
Food - 2 days   11,000 escudos
Ground transportation   7,000 escudos
                             TOTAL:

Madrid, Spain
Lodging - 2 nights   44,500 pesetas
Food - 3 days   16,000 pesetas
Ground transportation   6,000 pesetas
                             TOTAL:

Naples, Italy
Lodging - 2 nights   632,250 liras
Food - 3 days   210,000 liras
Ground transportation   85,000 liras
                             TOTAL:

Paris, France
Lodging - 3 nights   4,000 francs
Food - 4 days   1,600 francs
Ground transportation   N.A.   TOTAL:
                    TOTAL FOR TRIP, EXCLUDE AIR FARE: $

Please let me know if I can be of further assistance.

Sincerely,

Jill Kidd
Travel Agent

Inter-Office Memo

Karissa Jean's®

To: International Accountant

From: Bev Carter

Subject: Journalizing Payments and Receipts

Date: January 19, 19—

Listed below and on the following page are descriptions of sales and purchases between Karissa Jean's (made from the Denver office) and companies in foreign countries. Please record the transactions in Karissa Jean's International Accounting Journal (found on page 125). Date each entry using the date on which each transaction occurred.

January 8 — Sold jeans on account to Wallaby International of Australia for $45,000 (American dollars). The American dollar is the denominated currency. The direct quote for the Australian dollar was .7622 and the indirect quote was 1.3120.

January 9 — Purchased leather samples on account from CIA Mexicana Company of Mexico for 6,000 pesos. The Mexican peso is the denominated currency. The direct quote for pesos was .3206 and the indirect quote was 3.12.

January 10 — Sold jeans on account to Hasaki Corporation of Japan for $30,000 (American dollars). The American dollar is the denominated currency. The direct quote for the Japanese yen was .008148 and the indirect quote was 122.73.

January 11— Purchased fabric samples on account from Cheung Wan, Ltd. of Hong Kong for 3,200 Hong Kong dollars. The Hong Kong dollar is the denominated currency. The direct quote for the Hong Kong dollar was .12934 and the indirect quote was 7.7315.

Interoffice Memo
Journalizing Purchases and Sales
January 19, 19--
Page 2

January 12 — Purchased brass buttons on account from Mazzini SPA of Italy for 475,000 Italian liras. The Italian lira is the denominated currency. The direct quote for Italian lira was .0007619 and the indirect quote was 1312.59.

January 15 — Sold jeans on account to Newton-John, Ltd. of Australia for 16,500 Australian dollars. The Australian dollar is the denominated currency. The direct quote of Australian dollars was .7187 and the indirect quote was 1.3914.

January 16 — Purchased sample fabrics on account from Takatsu, Ltd. of Japan for 52,500 Japanese yen. The yen is the denominated currency. The direct quote for yen was .007994 and the indirect quote was 125.10.

January 17 — Sold jeans on account to Trans-World, Inc. of Canada for 18,000 Canadian dollars. The Canadian dollar is the denominated currency. The direct quote for the Canadian dollar was .8006 and the indirect quote was 1.2490.

Inter-Office Memo

To: International Accountant

From: Bev Carter

Subject: New Employee Training

Date: January 22, 19—

You will be pleased to know that you now have seniority in the International Accounting Department—we've just hired a new employee, Spence Blakeslee. He is now studying Karissa Jean's Training Manual. When he finishes the training program, Spence will be working primarily with Karissa Jean's foreign financial statements.

Since computing retained earnings is one of the more difficult concepts, I would like you to explain this process to Spence.

A consolidated form of Karissa Jean's France November trial balance is presented below. Please write Spence a memo describing the procedures and listing the steps he should follow to compute ending retained earnings. And, of course, compute the November 30 retained earnings as an example, listing titles and amounts. You can present the amounts in francs.

Karissa Jean's France

Trial Balance (in Francs)

November 30, 199--

Cash	2,072,813	
Other Assets	3,479,247	
Cost of Goods Sold	489,831	
Selling Expenses	203,576	
Administrative Expenses	89,045	
Dividends	17,410	
Accounts Payable		389,166
Notes Payable		1,744,119
Other Income		5,186
Sales		1,382,638
Retained Earnings, November 1, 19--		2,830,813
	6,351,922	6,351,922

Inter-Office Memo

To:

From:

Subject:

Date:

Inter-Office Memo

Karissa Jean's®

To: International Accountant

From: Bev Carter

Subject: Help

Date: January 29, 19—

Here's a letter we received from a Mexican company, Abamex, in Spanish. Since we're the *International* Accounting Department, the mail clerk routed it to us, of course!

Do me a favor, please. Find someone to translate this and route your translation to me. I'll pass it to the appropriate party.

Mucho Gracias!

Abamex Company
336 La Martine
Mexico, DF 11320

Karissa Jean's
8677 Colfax
Denver, Colorado 80227

Señoras Y Señores:

Hace unas semanas, cuando estuve en los Estados Unidos con mi negocio, compré un par de "Karissa's Jeans" para mi esposa como un regalo. A ella le gustan mucho, y dice que son los mejores bluejeans que ha tenido en su vida. Todas sus amigas la envidian y quieren comprar sus propios pares de jeans de Karissa.

Importo utensilios y electrodomésticos de los Estados Unidos, y los vendo por todo México. También estoy interasado en importar jeans de Karissa para venta en México. ¿Actualmente tienen Uds. un distribuidor en México? Si, no. ¿Considerarian dejar a mi compañia ser su distribuidor? También, por favor diganme el precio de cada par de los jeans de Karissa y la cantidad minima en cada orden.

Espero ansiosamente neustro futuro negocio.

Sinceramente,

Gregorio Lamente

TRANSLATION OF LETTER FROM ABAMEX COMPANY

Inter-Office Memo

To: International Accountant

From: Bev Carter

Subject: Journalizing Payments and Receipts

Date: February 19, 19—

Karissa Jean's®

Listed below and on the following page are descriptions of receipts and payments for transactions you recorded from my January 19 memo. Please record each receipt and payment in Karissa Jean's International Accounting Journal (found on page 125). You may need to refer to the January 19 memo and to your journal entries for additional information. Don't forget to record foreign exchange gains and losses where appropriate. Date each entry, using the date receipt or payment occurred.

February 8 —   Received payment from Wallaby International of Australia for our January 8 sale. The direct quote for the Australian dollar was .6878 and the indirect quote was 1.4539.

February 9 —   Paid CIA Mexicana Company of Mexico for our January 9 purchase. The direct quote for the Mexican peso was .3261 and the indirect quote was 3.067.

February 10 — Received payment from Hasaki Corporation of Japan for our January 10 sale. The direct quote for the Japanese yen was .008012 and the indirect quote was 124.82.

February 11— Paid Cheung Wan, Ltd. of Hong Kong for our January 11 purchase. The direct quote for the Hong Kong dollar was .12715 and the indirect quote was 7.7630.

February 12 — Paid Mazzini SPA of Italy for our January 12 purchase. The direct quote for Italian liras was .0006765 and the indirect quote was 1478.15.

Interoffice Memo
Journalizing Payments and Receipts
February 19, 19--
Page 2

February 15 – Received payment from Newton-John, Ltd. of Australia for our January 15 sale. The direct quote for the Australian dollar was .7439 and the indirect quote was 1.3443.

February 16 – Paid Takatsu, Ltd. of Japan for our January 16 purchase. The direct quote for the Japanese yen was .008210 and the indirect quote was 121.80.

February 17– Received payment from Trans-World, Inc. of Canada for our January 17 sale. The direct quote for the Canadian dollar was .7813 and the indirect quote was 1.2800.

Inter-Office Memo

Karissa Jean's®

To: International Accountant

From: Bev Carter

Subject: Outline for Presentation on International Accounting

Date: March 2, 19—

I've been asked to make a 50-minute presentation on international accounting at Arapahoe Community College in Littleton on Friday of next week. There will be approximately 40 Intermediate Accounting students in the class. Their instructor, Brock Matheason, informs me that their textbook contains about six pages of material on international accounting, which the students have not yet studied. The text provides no background information on international business.

Will you please develop an outline of topics and subtopics on international business and international accounting that I can use as a guide for my presentation? Since I'm limited to 50 minutes, I won't be able to tell them everything about international business and international accounting, so pick the most important topics. Also—make sure you have enough material so I don't run out with 20 minutes to go and end up standing there like an idiot!

Thanks for your help.

Outline

PRESENTATION ON INTERNATIONAL BUSINESS AND ACCOUNTING

Outline
International Business and Accounting
Page 2

Karissa Jean's® France

35 Rue De Flandre
Paris, Ville De P   75019

FAX TO: 01-303-721-7607

TO: International Accountant

FROM: Sean McMasters, Manager, Karissa Jean's France

DATE: March 8, 19--

Our accountant, Pierre, has fallen in love (third time this month), or as they say here, AMOUR. He seems to have great difficulty concentrating on his accounting duties and I am fearful that some of his work may be inaccurate. Therefore, I thought it may be best to have you review some of his work to see if he's on the right track.

Enclosed are descriptions of several transactions that are representative of the type we handle here, along with Pierre's journal entries. Please audit each entry. Since our next financial statements will be prepared on March 31, you will not need to be concerned about adjusting entries for unsettled foreign currency transactions. On the attached blank journal paper, please indicate the following:

1. If an entry is correct as shown by Pierre, show the date in your journal and write "okay" in the description.
2. If an error has been made in recording an entry, reverse Pierre's entry. Then record the entry that should have been made.
3. Please write a brief explanation after each correcting entry you make identifying what Pierre did wrong and what should have been done so Pierre can avoid similar errors in the future.

Remember, all transactions are recorded on our records in French francs. When converting from another foreign currency to francs or from francs to another foreign currency, always convert to American dollars first, and then convert to the other foreign currency or to francs. Thanks for your help.

Fax to International Accountant
From: Sean McMasters, Karissa Jean's France
Date: March 8
Page 2

Transactions
(Note: The currency exchange rates stated for each foreign currency are for converting to and from American dollars.)

February 1–   Sold jeans on account to a German company, Aschaffenburger GMBH for 10,000 German marks. The German mark is the denominated currency. The direct quote for German marks was .6177 and the indirect quote was 1.6190. The direct quote for the French franc was .18104 and the indirect quote was 5.5235.

February 2–   Purchased a photocopy machine on account from an Italian company, Piazzola SPA, for 3,683,351 Italian liras. The Italian lira is the denominated currency. The direct quote for the Italian lira was .0006787 and the indirect quote was 1473.34. The direct quote for the French franc was .18182 and the indirect quote was 5.500.

February 3–   Sold jeans on account to a British company, Lennon Garments, Inc., for 72,345 French francs. The french franc is the denominated currency. The direct quote for the British pound was 1.5325 and the indirect quote was .6525. The direct quote for the French franc was .17969 and the indirect quote was 5.5650.

February 4 – Purchased an office desk on account from a Danish company, Basballe, Inc., for 3,425 Danish kronen. The krone is the denominated currency. The direct quote for Danish kronen was .1606 and the indirect quote was 6.2286. The direct quote for the French franc was .18182 and the indirect quote was 5.500.

Fax to International Accountant
From: Sean McMasters, Karissa Jean's France
Date: March 8
Page 3

March 1 —   Received payment from Aschaffenburger
             GMBH from our February 1 sale. The direct
             quote for the German mark was .6341 and the
             indirect quote was 1.5770. The direct quote for
             the French franc was .18824 and the indirect
             quote was 5.3125.

March 2 —   Paid Piazzolla SPA for our February 2 pur-
             chase. The direct quote for the Italian lira was
             .0008870 and the indirect quote was 1127.34.
             The direct quote for the French franc was
             .19980 and the indirect quote was 5.0050.

March 3 —   Received payment from Lennon Garments,
             Inc., from our February 3 sale. The direct
             quote for the British pound was 1.9220 and the
             indirect quote was .5203. The direct quote for
             the French franc was .19972 and the indirect
             quote was 5.0180.

March 4 —   Paid Basballe, Inc., for our February 4 pur-
             chase. The direct quote for the Danish krone
             was .1696 and the indirect quote was 5.8950.
             The direct quote for the French franc was
             .19337 and the indirect quote was 5.1715.

Karissa Jean's France
Journal   Page

Date	Description	Post Ref.	Debit	Credit
Feb. 1	Accounts Receivable / Aschffenburger GmbH		6,177.00	
	Sales			6,177.00
Feb. 2	Office Equipment		13,749.40	
	Accounts Payable / Piazzolla SPA			13,749.40
Feb. 3	Accounts Receivable / Lennon Garants, Inc		72,345.00	
	Sales			72,345.00
Feb. 4	Office Equipment		100.01	
	Accounts Payable / Basballe, Inc			100.01

Date	Description	Post Ref.	Debit	Credit
Mar. 1	Cash		33,686.56	
	Foreign Exchange Gain			27,509.56
	Accounts Receivable / Aschffenburger GmbH			6,177.00
Mar. 2	Accounts Payable / Piazzolla SPA		13,749.40	
	Cash			13,749.40
Mar. 3	Cash		72,345.00	
	Accounts Payable / Lennon Garants, Inc.			72,345.00
Mar. 4	Accounts Payable / Basballe, Inc.		100.01	
	Foreign Exchange Loss		12.31	
	Cash			112.32

Karissa Jean's France
Journal

Page _____

Date	Description	Post. Ref.	Debit	Credit

Karissa Jean's France Journal

Page

Date	Description	Post. Ref.	Debit	Credit

Karissa Jean's France Journal

Page

Date	Description	Post. Ref.	Debit	Credit

Inter-Office Memo

Karissa Jean's®

To: International Accountant

From: Bev Carter

Subject: Study of Proposed System to Avoid Foreign Currency Exchange Losses

Date: March 16, 19--

Usually, when we purchase goods from a company in a foreign country, we are required to make payment in that foreign company's currency.

Normally, we buy on account, with payment to be made 30 to 60 days after the purchase. Because of these deferred payments, we usually experience a foreign currency exchange gain or loss when payment is made. In essence, this amounts to speculating in the foreign currency market. If we're lucky, we experience a gain–an unearned windfall. If we're unlucky, we experience a loss–an underserved expense.

Since we're a business and not a speculator, I'd like to find a way to take the currency exchange risks out of our business dealings.

On the attached sheet is a list of several purchases we made last year, along with the currency exchange rates that existed on the purchase date and payment date. I wonder if we would have gained or lost money if we had done the following:

1. On the purchase date, buy the foreign currency that will be needed for payment 30 to 60 days hence on the payment date.
2. On the purchase date, borrow the money needed to buy the foreign currency, so we don't tie up our own capital. We would repay the loan on the scheduled payment date, so the loan would be for the credit period, 30 to 60 days.
3. On the purchase date, invest the foreign currency we have bought and leave it invested the 30 to 60 days until the payment date.

Interoffice Memo
Study of Proposed System to Avoid Foreign Currency
    Exchange Losses
March 16, 19--
Page 2

4. On the payment date, pay the amount due, using the foreign currency we bought on the purchase date.

Please complete the attached chart, calculating the following:

1. The currency exchange gain or loss we would have experienced if we had simply waited until the payment date to make payment, which is the procedure we currently follow.
2. The interest expense for borrowing the money to buy the foreign currency on the purchase date. The loan period will be the number of days in the credit period. Use a 12 percent interest rate and a 365-day year. Remember, the formula for calculating interest is as follows:

$$\text{Principal} \times \text{Rate} \times \text{Time} = \text{Interest}$$

3. The interest income earned from investing the foreign currency from the purchase date to the payment date. This will be the number of days in the credit period. Use a 5 percent interest rate on the investment and a 365-day year. Use the same interest formula as that used to calculate interest on loans. Be sure to convert the interest earned on the foreign currency investment back to American dollars. You can use the currency exchange rate on the payment date.
4. The net interest income or expense, computed by determining the difference between interest income earned by investing the foreign currency and the interest expense on our loan to buy foreign currency. Since this may sound a little confusing, I've done the first calculation for you.

Interoffice Memo
Study of Proposed System to Avoid Foreign Currency
   Exchange Losses
March 16, 19--
Page 3

1. Calculate exchange gain or loss.
    A. Convert marks to American dollars on date of purchase.
       15,000 × .6297 = $9,445.50
    B. Convert marks to American dollars on date of payment.
       15,000 × .6727 = $10,090.50
    C. Calculate the foreign currency exchange gain or loss.
       $10,090.50 − $9,445.50 = $645.00 Loss
2. Calculate interest expense on the loan to borrow $9,445.50 at
   12 percent to purchase 15,000 marks on the purchase date. The
   loan period is the 30 days in the credit period.
       Principal × Rate × Time = Interest
       $9,445.50 × 12 percent × 30/365 = $93.16
3. Calculate interest earned on the 15,000 marks at 5 percent for
   30 days.
       Principal × Rate × Time = Interest
       15,000 × 5 percent × 30/365 = 61.64 marks
       (marks)
4. Convert the interest earned in marks to American dollars using
   the direct quote on the payment date.
       61.64 marks × .6727 = $41.47
5. Calculate the net interest income or net interest expense.

Interest Expense on Loan:	$93.16
Less Interest Income on Investment	−41.47
Net Interest Expense:	$51.69

To determine the effectiveness of this proposed technique, we
need to compare the foreign currency exchange gain or loss that
would result from our current procedure to the net interest income
or expense that would result from the proposed procedure.

Interoffice Memo
Study of Proposed System to Avoid Foreign Currency
    Exchange Losses
March 16, 19--
Page 4

As you can see in this example, an exchange loss of $645.00 would result if we used our current procedure, purchasing the 15,000 German marks on the payment date. If we had used the proposed technique, purchasing the marks on the purchase date, we would have had no exchange loss and we would have had only a net interest expense of $51.69. Thus, by using the proposed technique, we would incur $593.31 less of a loss ($645.00 – $51.69). It will be interesting to see how the other calculations work out.

	Purchase Amount	Days in Credit Period	Currency Exchange Rate Date of Purchase (Direct Quote)	Currency Exchange Rate Date of Payment (Direct Quote)	Exchange Gain or Loss	Interest Expense on Loan	Interest Income on Invest. (American Dollars)	Net Interest Income or Expense
1.	15,000 German marks	30	.6297	.6727	$645.00 Loss	$93.16	$41.47	$51.69 Expense
2.	450,000 Japanese yen	60	.007893	.007675				
3.	25,000 Mexican pesos	60	.3269	.3202				
4.	20,000 Canadian dollars	60	.7803	.7895				

International Accountant: In the space below, describe whether or not this proposed technique would be worth following.

Inter-Office Memo

Karissa Jean's®

To: International Accountant

From: Bev Carter

Subject: Quarter-Ending Adjusting Entries

Date: April 5, 19--

Shown below is a summary of our foreign currency purchases and sales on account that were unsettled as of our March 31 quarter end. The foreign company's currency is the denominated currency in each transaction.

Please record the March 31 adjusting entry showing the foreign exchange gain or loss for each transaction in Karissa Jean's International Accounting Journal.

Transaction	Company Name	Country Company From	Amount	Currency Exchange Rates (Direct Quote)	
				Transaction Date	March 31
Purchase	Gustav, Inc.	Austria	15,000 schillings	.08944	.09585
Purchase	Treynor, Inc.	Hungary	388,000 forints	.0129166	.0128785
Sale	Korosaki Co.	Japan	675,000 yen	.008210	.007893
Sale	Wyndham Co.	Australia	40,000 Australian dollars	.7609	.7645
Purchase	Pokeva Co.	Finland	11,000 markkas	.22185	.21876

Karissa Jean's® France

35 Rue De Flandre
Paris, Ville De P 75019

    TO: Beverly Carter, Manager, International Accounting Department

    FROM: Sean McMasters, Manager, Karissa Jean's France

    RE: Financial Statement Translation

DATE: April 11, 19--

    Enclosed are the income statement, retained earnings statement, and

balance sheet for Karissa Jean's France for January - March, with amounts

shown in francs, of course. After receiving some assistance from the

international accountant in your office, I believe our accountant, Pierre,

is now back on track (accounting wise - his love life is still a mess) and that

all of the information presented in our financial statements is correct.

    It will be interesting to see what these statements translate to in

American dollars. Please forward a copy as soon as translation is completed.

To: International Accountant:
    Congratulations on surviving your first three months in Karissa Jean's international accounting department. And, thanks for all your help. But, before we cut the cake, I've got a "final test" for you.

    Please translate the following financial statements for Karissa Jean's France into American dollars using the translation information I've provided for you on the attached sheet. Round your answers to the nearest dollar. Present your translated financial statements in good form using the attached accounting papers.

                                    Thanks,
                                    Bev

Karissa Jean's France
Income Statement (in Francs)
For Three Months Ending March 31, 19--

		(in Francs)
Sales		3,791,526
Cost of Goods Sold		−1,592,439
Gross Profit		2,199,087

Selling Expenses:
Sales Commissions	265,407	
Advertising	151,662	
Travel	47,397	
Telephone	22,749	
Sales Salaries Expense	245,187	
Total Selling Expenses		732,402

Administrative Expenses:
Rent	45,000	
Insurance	26,541	
Depreciation	11,175	
Administrative Salaries	157,419	
Total Administrative Expenses		240,135

| Total Operating Expenses | | 972,537 |
| Net Income | | 1,226,550 |

Karissa Jean's France
Retained Earnings Statement (in Francs)
For Three Months Ending March 31, 19--

	(in Francs)
Retained Earnings, January 1, 19--	2,409,420
Add Net Income	1,226,550
Less Dividends	76,881
Retained Earnings, March 31, 19--	3,559,089

Karissa Jean's France
Balance Sheet (in Francs)
March 31, 19--

<u>Assets</u>   (in Francs)

     Cash in Bank 2,557,257
     Accounts Receivable 1,591,092
     Merchandise Inventory 849,657
     Office Equipment & Furniture (Net) 920,172

     Total Assets 5,918,178

<u>Liabilities</u>

     Accounts Payable 435,639
     Notes Payable 1,623,450

     Total Liabilities 2,059,089

<u>Stockholder's Equity</u>

     Common Stock 300,000
     Retained Earnings 3,559,089

     Total Stockholder's Equity 3,859,089

     Total Liabilities & Stockholder's Equity 5,918,178

International Accountant: Here's the translation information for translating Karissa Jean's France financial statements. Bev

Translation Information

(Currency Exchange Rates Show Direct Quote of French Franc)

Current Rate, March 31	.18824
Weighted-Average for January - March	.18106
Rate on Dividend Declaration Date	.18782
Rate on Date Karissa Jean's France Was Established	.15457
Beginning Translated Retained Earnings (in American Dollars)	$409,359

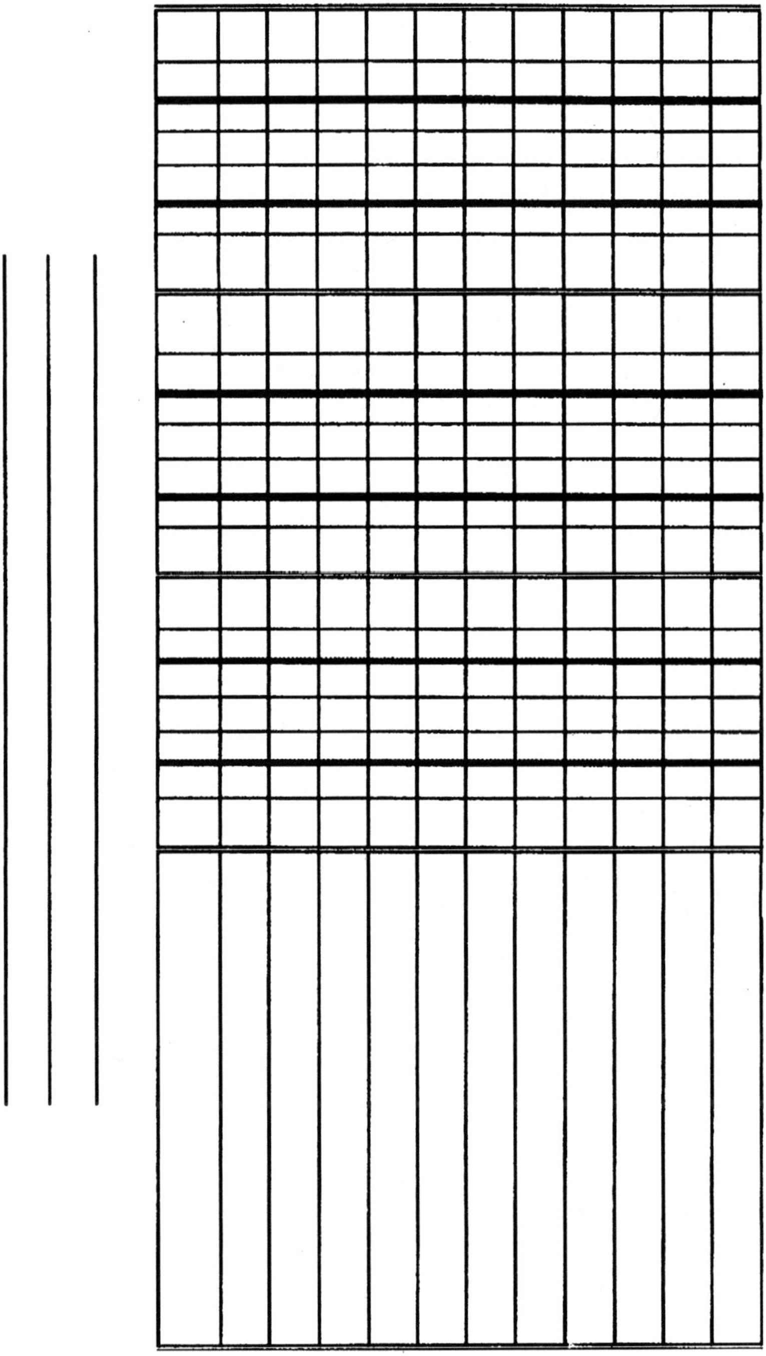

(continued)

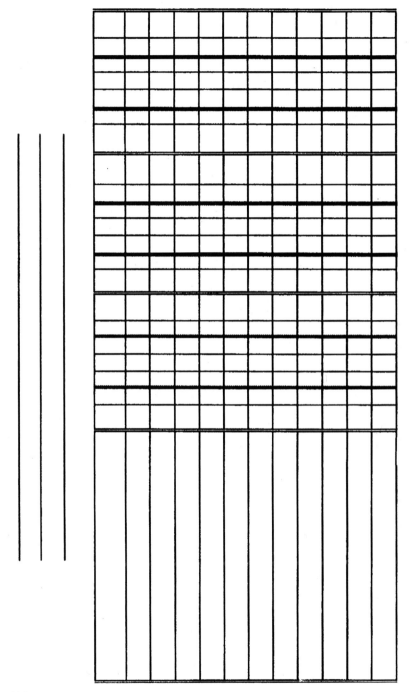

(continued)

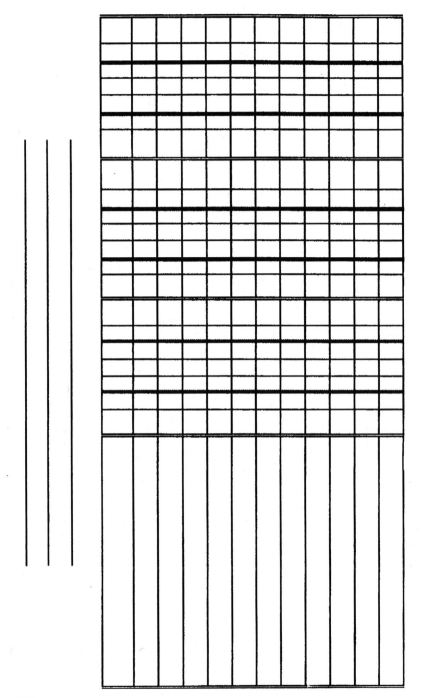

Inter-Office Memo

Karissa Jean's®

To: International Accountant

From: Bev Carter

Subject: Four-Month Review

Date: May 11, 19--

Time flies–you've now been at Karissa Jean's for four months and it's time for your first review. Selected activities you've performed in the International Accounting Department will be reviewed and evaluated. Follow your immediate supervisor's instructions for providing information, based on transactions you've recorded and activities you've performed.

Your salary adjustment and future job placement within the International Accounting Department will be based on the results of this review. Since you've done so well in all of your activities, I'm sure your review will be very satisfactory.

Karissa Jean's®

International Accounting Journal

International Journal

Page

Date	Description	Post. Ref.	Debit	Credit

International Journal

Page _____

Date	Description	Post. Ref.	Debit	Credit

128

International Journal

Date	Description	Post. Ref.	Debit	Credit

Page

130

International Journal   Page _____

Date	Description	Post. Ref.	Debit	Credit

Date	Description	Post. Ref.	Debit	Credit

International Journal   Page

International Journal

Date	Description	Post. Ref.	Debit	Credit

Page

International Journal

Date	Description	Post. Ref.	Debit	Credit

Page

International Journal

Page ____

Date	Description	Post. Ref.	Debit	Credit

Index

Karissa Jean's®

An International Accounting Practice Set

Instructor's Manual
and
Answer Key

The Haworth Press, Inc., 10 Alice Street, Binghamton, NY 13904-1580

CONTENTS

INTRODUCTION

American companies are becoming increasingly involved in international business activities. This involvement has created the need for students pursuing a career in business and accounting to become familiar with international business operations and international accounting procedures.

An International Accounting Practice Set: The Karissa Jean's Simulation provides business and accounting students with training and experience in international business and international accounting.

PRACTICE SET DESIGN

The student assumes the role of a newly hired employee in the International Accounting Department of Karissa Jean's, an international distributor of men's and women's jeans. In this role, the student first participates in Karissa Jean's training program in international business and international accounting. After completing the training program, the student performs as an international accountant in Karissa Jean's International Accounting Department. The practice set is divided into two sections, the *Training Manual* and the *Simulation*.

TRAINING MANUAL

Karissa Jean's Training Manual describes international business operations and international accounting procedures. It presents all of the information the student will need to know to complete the simulation, where they assume the role of an international accountant. The Training Manual contains the following features.

Background Information. The Training Manual starts in the beginning, describing international business, ways to enter foreign markets, obstacles to international trade, international trade organizations, and international accounting practices. After studying this information, the student should have a good understanding of international business practices and international accounting procedures.

Practice Problems. An example and step-by-step solution follow the explanation of each international accounting procedure. Practice problems are presented for the students to apply what they have learned.

Progress Tests. The Training Manual contains three self-tests, called *progress tests*, for the students to measure their comprehension of the material presented. These are presented at intervals in the Training Manual.

Training Manual Answers. Answers to the practice problems and progress tests are presented in the back of the Training Manual for the students to measure the accuracy of their answers and to verify their procedures. Step-by-step calculations show how the answers were determined.

Simulation

After completing the Training Manual, the student reports for work in Karissa Jean's International Accounting Department. Here, the student receives instructions, via memos, for transactions they are to record and activities they are to perform.

The intent of the simulation is to provide students with not only experience in recording international accounting transactions, but also to provide them with experience in problem solving and writing. Activities included in the simulation include the following:

1. Convert foreign currencies to American dollars.
2. Convert American dollars to foreign currencies.
3. Convert one foreign currency to another foreign currency.
4. Record international sales, purchases, cash receipts, and cash payments in an American company's general journal.
5. Record international sales, purchases, cash receipts, and cash payments in a foreign marketing subsidiary general journal.
6. Record adjusting entries for unsettled accounts payable and accounts receivable at the end of an accounting period.
7. Describe in a memo the procedure for computing retained earnings.

8. Translate a letter from Spanish to English. (Note: The student may need to locate outside assistance for this.)
9. Prepare an outline for a speech to be presented on international business and international accounting.
10. Audit Karissa Jean's French marketing subsidiary journal and identify and correct any errors.
11. Translate foreign financial statements from French francs to American dollars.

Only two activities in the simulation are interdependent—the January 19 and February 19 memos. Each of the other activities are unrelated and any of them may be eliminated at the instructor's discretion.

Exams

Two exams are provided in this instructor's manual to measure student comprehension and performance.

Training Exam. The training exam covers material presented in the training manual portion of the practice set. It is designed to be administered after students have completed the training manual and before they complete the simulation. It measures the student's comprehension of international business and international accounting practices.

Performance Review. The performance review calls for the students to provide their answers from transactions recorded and activities performed in the simulation. It is a handy way for the instructor to check the student's performance on the simulation without checking each individual activity.

STUDENT SKILLS REQUIRED

The student needs no prior knowledge of international business or international accounting to complete this practice set. All of the necessary information is presented to the student in the training manual section of the practice set.

Only a basic understanding of accounting principles is required and this practice set may be used anytime after the first quarter or first semester of accounting principles. Students will need to have a general understanding of the following to complete the practice set:

1. Record sales, purchases, cash payments, and cash receipts in a general journal.
2. Record basic adjusting entries in a general journal.
3. Understand the basic principles involved in completing an income statement, retained earnings statement, and balance sheet.

SUGGESTED USES OF THIS PRACTICE SET

An International Accounting Practice Set: The Karissa Jean's Simulation can be used in a wide variety of situations, including the following:

- Supplement to any accounting course, such as accounting principles or intermediate accounting.
- Individualized study project for any accounting or business student.
- Extra credit assignment.
- Honors student assignment.
- Project for interim class.
- Short course in international business and/or international accounting.
- Supplement to international business course.
- Training program for multinational corporation or for any company engaged in international business.

ANSWERS TO SIMULATION

Answers to activities in the simulation are presented here chronologically by date of the memos in the simulation. However, the January 19, February 19, and April 5 memos call for recording journal entries in the Karissa Jean's International Accounting Journal and those entries are found at the end of this answer section.

World-Wide Travel Agency, Inc.
3610 Chambers
Aurora, CO 80245

January 15, 19--

Ms. Karissa Fowler
KARISSA JEAN'S
8677 Colfax Avenue
Denver, CO 80227

Dear Ms. Fowler:

This is to confirm our earlier telephone conversation about
your inquiry for the following flight itinerary: Denver -
Dublin, Ireland - Lisbon, Portugal - Madrid, Spain - Naples,
Italy - Paris, France - Denver. The first-class flight is
$3,149. Other costs you inquired about are estimated below:

CONVERTED TO AMERICAN $

Dublin, Ireland
Lodging - 2 nights	205 punt	$ 347.39
Food - 3 days	70 punt	118.62
Ground transportation	30 punt	50.84
	TOTAL:	$ 516.85

Lisbon, Portugal
Lodging - 1 night	25,000 escudos	179.43
Food - 2 days	11,000 escudos	78.95
Ground transportation	7,000 escudos	50.24
	TOTAL:	$ 308.62

Madrid, Spain
Lodging - 2 nights	44,500 pesetas	400.77
Food - 3 days	16,000 pesetas	144.10
Ground transportation	6,000 pesetas	54.04
	TOTAL:	$ 598.91

Naples, Italy
Lodging - 2 nights	632,250 liras	450.04
Food - 3 days	210,000 liras	149.48
Ground transportation	85,000 liras	60.50
	TOTAL:	$ 660.02

Paris, France
Lodging - 3 nights	4,000 francs	750.84
Food - 4 days	1,600 francs	300.34
Ground transportation	N.A.	TOTAL:	$1,051.18

TOTAL FOR TRIP, EXCLUDE AIR FARE: $3,135.58

Please let me know if I can be of further assistance.

Sincerely,

Jill Kidd
Travel Agent

Inter-Office Memo

Karissa Jean's®

To: Spence Blakeslee

From: (Student Name)

Subject: Procedure for Computing Retained Earnings

Date: (Solution to January 22 Memo)

(NOTE TO INSTRUCTOR: Student wording will vary, but students should describe why they're writing the memo and should identify the following:)

1. Beginning retained earnings is taken directly from the trial balance.

2. Net income is computed as follows: Sales + Other Income
   − Cost of Goods Sold
   − Selling and
     Administrative Expenses
   = Net Income or Net Loss

3. The dividend amount is taken from the trial balance. It may be wise to identify that the dividend is not an expense, but rather, is a distribution of net income to the stockholders.

––––––––––

(Following is a sample of what might be contained in the student memo.)

Beverly Carter asked me to identify the procedures and steps to follow in computing retained earnings for a retained earnings statement. She provided me with the attached copy of Karissa Jean's France November 30 trial balance. The procedures to follow in calculating retained earnings and the retained earnings statement, completed from the trial balance data, are shown below.

Karissa Jean's France
Retained Earnings Statement (in Francs)
November 30, 19--

```
Retained Earnings, November 1, 19-- .....    2,830,813
Add Net Income ......................    +  605,372
Less Dividends .......................    -   17,410

Retained Earnings, November 30, 19-- ......    3,418,775
```

Translation of Letter from Abamex Company

Ladies and Gentlemen:

When I was in the United States on business a few weeks ago, I purchased a pair of Karissa's jeans for my wife as a present. She likes them very much and says they are the finest jeans she has ever owned. All of her friends envy her and want to buy some Karissa's jeans for themselves.

I import housewares from the United States and sell them throughout Mexico. I am also interested in importing Karissa's jeans for sale in Mexico. Do you currently have a Mexican distributor? If you do not, would you consider allowing my company to become your distributor? Also, please tell me what my cost would be per pair of Karissa's jeans and what the minimum quantity per order would be.

I am looking forward to doing business with you.

Sincerely,
(Signed)
Gregorio Lamente

NOTE TO INSTRUCTOR: Most likely, student translations will not be a word-for-word copy of the translation shown here. Grade student answers only on *content* and *meaning* rather than a word-for-word translation.

(Solution to March 2 Memo)

Outline
PRESENTATION ON INTERNATIONAL BUSINESS AND ACCOUNTING

(Student answers will vary, but the outline for Beverly Carter's presentation to the Arapahoe Community College intermediate accounting class should probably include most of the following. This outline parallels topics presented in Karissa Jean's Training Manual. It will be interesting to see if students include additional topics like Item VI on this possible solution, Careers in International Accounting.)

I. Definition of International Business
   A. Balance of Trade
      1. Exports
      2. Imports
      3. Trade Surplus
      4. Trade Deficit
   B. Balance of Payments

II. Ways to Enter Foreign Markets
   A. Exporting
      1. Direct Exporting
      2. Indirect Exporting
   B. Licensing
   C. Franchising
   D. Joint Venture
   E. Marketing Subsidiary
   F. Contract Manufacturing
   G. Wholly Owned Subsidiary

III. Obstacles to International Trade
   A. Cultural Differences
      1. Customs, Religions, etc.
   B. Language Differences
      1. Problem with Translation, Connotations, etc.
      2. Potential Packaging and Labeling Problems
   C. Economic Conditions
      1. High Rate of Inflation in Some Countries
      2. Limited Purchasing Power in Some Countries

D. Marketing Difficulties
   1. Difficulty in Assembling Market Research Data
   2. Inferior Infrastructure Makes Communication and
      Distribution Difficult
E. Fluctuating Currency Exchange Rates
   1. Describe Currency Exchange Rates
   2. Describe Sales on Credit and Exchange Gains and Losses
   3. Describe Strong Dollar and Weak Dollar
F. Foreign Government Instability
   1. Revolutions, Drastic Foreign Policy Changes, etc.
G. Trade Protectionism
   1. Import Quotas
   2. Tariffs
   3. Embargoes
   4. Export Subsidies
   5. Retaliation

IV. International Trade Organizations
    A. Economic Communities
       1. European Community
    B. Cartels
       1. OPEC

V. International Accounting Activities
   A. Foreign Currency Financial Transactions
      1. Purchase and Sale of Goods on Account with
         American Dollar as Denominated Currency
      2. Purchase and Sale of Goods on Account with Foreign
         Currency as Denominated Currency
         a. Recognizing Foreign Currency Exchange Gain or
            Loss upon Payment or Receipt of Payment
   B. Foreign Currency Transactions Adjustment
      1. Unsettled Accounts Receivable or Accounts Payable at
         End of Accounting Period
   C. Foreign Currency Financial Statements
      1. Foreign Subsidiary Records Transactions and
         Financial Statements in Their Own Currency
      2. Translation of Foreign Subsidiary Financial Statements
         to American Dollar

VI. Careers in International Accounting
    A. Education Recommended
    B. Employment Possibilities
    C. On-the-Job Activities
    D. Salary Potential

Karissa Jean's France
Journal

Page

Date	Description	Post Ref.	Debit	Credit
Feb. 1	Sales		6,177.00	
	Accounts Receivable/Aschaffenburger GMBH			6,177.00
	(Reverses erroneous entry)			
Feb. 1	Accounts Receivable/Aschaffenburger GMBH		34,118.66	
	Sales			34,118.66
	(To record correct entry. Pierre's amount, 6,177.00, was marks converted to American dollars. Then, the dollars must be converted to francs by multiplying by indirect quote of the franc, 5.5235)			
Feb. 2	Okay			

10

Date	Description	Debit	Credit
Feb. 3	Okay		
Feb. 4	Accounts Payable/Basballe, Inc.	100.01	
	Office Equipment		100.01
	(Reverses erroneous entry)		
Feb. 4	Office Equipment	3,025.33	
	Accounts Payable/Basballe, Inc.		3,025.33
	(To record correct entry. Pierre correctly converted Danish krone to American dollars, but used the direct quote for francs to convert American dollars to francs. He should have used the indirect quote, 5.500, to convert American dollars to French francs.		

Karissa Jean's France
Journal

Page

Date	Description	Post Ref.	Debit	Credit
Mar. 1	Accounts Receivable/Aschaffenburger GMBH		6,177.00	
	Foreign Exchange Gain		27,509.56	
	Cash			33,686.56
	(To reverse erroneous entry)			
Mar. 1	Cash		33,686.56	
	Foreign Exchange Loss		432.10	
	Accounts Receivable/Aschaffenburger GMBH			34,118.66
	(To record correct entry. Pierre recorded correct cash receipt amount,			
	but error in recording the February 1 sale led to recording other parts of			
	the entry incorrectly.)			

Date	Account	Debit	Credit
Mar. 2	Cash	13,749.40	
	Accounts Payable/Piazzolla SPA		13,749.40
	(To reverse erroneous entry)		
Mar. 2	Accounts Payable/Piazzolla SPA	13,749.40	
	Foreign Exchange Loss	2,602.60	
	Cash		16,352.00
	(To record correct entry. Pierre failed to calculate the currency exchange on the Mar. 2 payment date and failed to recognize the foreign exchange loss caused by deferred payment.)		
Mar. 3	Accounts Payable/Lennon Garments, Inc.	72,345.00	
	Cash		72,345.00
	(To reverse erroneous entry)		

13

Karissa Jean's France
Journal

Page

Date	Description	Post Ref.	Debit	Credit
Mar. 3	Cash		72,345.00	
	Accounts Rec./Lennon Garments, Inc.			72,345.00
	(To record correct entry. Pierre credited accounts payable instead of accounts receivable.)			
Mar. 4	Cash		112.32	
	Accounts Payable/Basballe, Inc.			100.01
	Foreign Exchange Loss			12.31
	(To reverse erroneous entry)			

Date	Account	Debit	Credit
Mar. 4	Accounts Payable/Basballe, Inc.	3,025.33	
	Foreign Exchange Gain		21.31
	Cash		3,004.02
	(To record correct entry. Pierre made same error in currency conversion as he made Feb. 4 to record the purchase. That is, Danish krone was correctly converted to American dollars, but he used the direct quote, instead of indirect quote, to convert American dollars to French francs.)		

15

Solution to March 16 Memo

	Purchase Amount	Days in Credit Period	Currency Exchange Rate Date of Purchase (Direct Quote)	Currency Exchange Rate Date of Payment (Direct Quote)	Exchange Gain or Loss	Interest Expense on Loan	Interest Income on Invest. (American Dollars)	Net Interest Income or Expense
1.	15,000 German marks	30	.6297	.6727	$645.00 Loss	$93.16	$41.47	$51.69 Expense
2.	450,000 Japanese yen	60	.007893	.007675	$98.10 Gain	$70.06	$28.39	$41.67 Expense
3.	25,000 Mexican pesos	60	.3269	.3202	$167.50 Gain	$161.21	$65.79	$95.42 Expense
4.	20,000 Canadian dollars	60	.7803	.7895	$184.00 Loss	$307.84	$129.78	$178.06 Expense

International Accountant: In the space below, describe whether or not this proposed technique would be worth following.

(Student answers will vary, but the following concepts should be presented:)

1. If an exchange gain would result, the current procedure would be the best to use (as in items 2 and 3).
2. If a large exchange loss would occur, the proposed procedure would limit the overall loss to a smaller amount (as in item 1).
3. If a small exchange loss would occur, the proposed procedure would limit the overall loss to a smaller amount (as in item 4).
4. In summary, the comparative results of the proposed procedure are still determined by currency fluctuations. It may be wise to investigate a different form of hedging.

Solution to April 11 Memo - Financial Statement Translation

Karissa Jean's France
Income Statement (in Dollars)
For Three Months Ending March 31, 19--   (Procedure)

Sales	$686,494	(3,791,526 francs × .18106)
Cost of Goods Sold	288,327	(1,592,439 francs × .18106)
Gross Profit	$398,167	(Sales − Cost of Goods Sold)

Selling Expenses:

Sales Commissions	$48,055	(265,407 francs × .18106)
Advertising	27,460	(151,662 francs × .18106)
Travel	8,582	(47,397 francs × .18106)
Telephone	4,119	(22,749 francs × .18106)
Sales Salaries	44,394	(245,187 francs × .18106)
Total Selling Expenses	$132,610	(Total of Sales Expense
Amts.)		

Administrative Expenses:

Rent	8,148	(45,000 francs × .18106)
Insurance	4,806	(26,541 francs × .18106)
Depreciation	2,023	(11,175 francs × .18106)
Administrative Salaries.	28,502	(157,419 francs x .18106)
Total Administrataive Expenses	$ 43,479	(Total of Admin. Exp. Amounts)
Total Operating Expenses	*$176,089	(Selling Exp. + Admin. Exp.)
Net Income	$222,078	(Gross Profit − Total Exp.)

* Because of rounding, total operating expenses, calculated by adding the translated amounts in dollars is $1 more than that which results from translating total operating expenses from francs to dollars.

Karissa Jean's France
Retained Earnings Statement (in Dollars)
For Three Months Ending March 31, 19--   (Procedure)

Retained Earnings, January 1 ..	$409,359	(From Translation Information)
Add: Net Income	222,078	(From March 31 Inc. Statement)
Less: Dividends	14,440	(76,881 francs × .18782)
Retained Earnings, March 31 ..	$616,997	(Jan. 1 R.E. + N.I. − Divid.)

Karissa Jean's France
Balance Sheet (in Dollars)
March 31, 19--

Assets		(Procedure)
Cash in Bank	$ 481,378	(2,557,257 francs × .18824)
Accounts Receivable	299,507	(1,591,092 francs × .18824)
Merchandise Inventory	159,939	(849,657 francs × .18824)
Office Equip. & Furn. (Net)	173,213	(920,172 francs × .18824)
Total Assets	$1,114,037	(Total of Asset Amounts)

Liabilities		
Accounts Payable	$ 82,005	(435,639 francs × .18824)
Notes Payable	305,598	(1,623,450 francs × .18824)
Total Liabilities	$ 387,603	(Total of Liability Amounts)

Stockholder's Equity		
Common Stock	$ 46,371	(300,000 francs × .15457)
Retained Earnings	616,997	(From March 31 R.E. Stmt.)
Add: Trans. Adjustment	63,066	(To Balance Balance Sheet)
Total Stockholder's Equity	$ 726,434	(Total of Stk. Equity Amts.)
Total Liabilities and Stockholder's Equity	$1,114,037	(After Translation Adjustment, Assets = Liab. + Stk. Equity)

Karissa Jean's®

International Accounting Journal

International Journal					Page 1
Date	Description	Post Ref.	Debit	Credit	
	(Solutions To January 19 Memo)				
Jan. 8	Accounts Receivable/Wallaby International		45,000.00		
	Sales			45,000.00	
	(Since American dollar is the denominated currency, record sale in American dollars)				
Jan. 9	Purchases		1,923.60		
	Accounts Payable/CIA Mexicana Company			1,923.60	
	(6,000 pesos x .3206 = $1,923.60)				
Jan. 10	Accounts Receivable/Hasaki Corporation		30,000.00		

Date	Account	Debit	Credit
	Sales		30,000.00
	(Since American dollar is the denominated currency, record sale in American dollars.)		
Jan. 11	Purchases	413.89	
	Accounts Payable/Cheung Wan, Ltd.		413.89
	(3,200 Hong Kong dollars x .12934 = $413.89)		
Jan. 12	Purchases	361.90	
	Accounts Payable/Mazzini SPA		361.90
	(475,000 Italian liras x .0007619 = $361.90)		
Jan. 15	Accounts Receivable/Newton-John, Ltd.	11,858.55	
	Sales		11,858.55
	(16,500 Australian dollars x .7187 = $11,858.55)		

International Journal

Date	Description	Post Ref.	Debit	Credit
Jan. 16	Purchases		419.69	
	Accounts Payable/Takatsu, Ltd.			419.69
	(52,500 Japanese yen x .007994 = $419.69)			
Jan. 17	Accounts Receivable/Trans-World, Inc.		14,410.80	
	Sales			14,410.80
	(18,000 Canadian dollars x .8006 = $14,410.80)			
	(Solutions To February 19 Memo)			
Feb. 8	Cash		45,000.00	

Date	Account / Description		
	Accounts Receivable/Wallaby International		45,000.00
	(Since American dollar is the denominated currency, record cash receipt in American dollars.)		
Feb. 9	Accounts Payable/CIA Mexicana Company	1,923.60	
	Foreign Exchange Loss	33.00	
	Cash		1,956.60
	(6,000 pesos x .3261 = $1,956.60 payment due. Jan. 9 purchase was recorded for $1,923.60. $1,956.60 - $1,923.60 = $33.00 loss)		
Feb. 10	Cash	30,000.00	
	Accounts Receivable/Hasaki Corporation		30,000.00
	(Since American dollar is the denominated currency, record cash receipt in American dollars.)		

International Journal				Page 3	
Date	Description	Post Ref.	Debit	Credit	
Feb. 11	Accounts Payable/Cheung Wan, Ltd.		413.89		
	Foreign Exchange Gain			7.01	
	Cash			406.88	
	(3,200 Hong Kong dollars x .12715 = $406.88 payment due. Jan. 11 purchase				
	was recorded for $413.89. $413.89 - $406.88 = $7.01 gain)				
Feb. 12	Accounts Payable/Mazzini SPA		361.90		
	Foreign Exchange Gain			40.56	
	Cash			321.34	
	(475,000 Italian lira x .0006765 = $321.34 payment due. Jan. 12 purchase				
	was recorded for $361.90. $361.90 - $321.34 = $40.56 gain)				

Date	Account	Debit	Credit
Feb. 15	Cash	12,274.35	
	Foreign Exchange Gain		415.80
	Accounts Receivable/Newton-John, Ltd.		11,858.55
	(16,500 Australian dollars x .7439 = $12,274.35. Jan. 15 sale was recorded for $11,858.55. $12,274.35 - $11,858.55 = $415.80 gain)		
Feb. 16	Accounts Payable/Takatsu, Ltd.	419.69	
	Foreign Exchange Loss	11.34	
	Cash		431.03
	(52,500 Japanese yen x .008210 = $431.03. Jan. 16 purchase was recorded for $419.69. $431.03 - $419.69 = $11.34 loss)		

International Journal

Page 4

Date	Description	Post Ref.	Debit	Credit
Feb. 17	Cash		14,063.40	
	Foreign Exchange Loss		347.40	
	Accounts Receivable/Trans-World, Inc.			14,410.80
	(18,000 Canadian dollars x .7813 = $14,063.40. Jan. 17 sale was recorded			
	for $14,410.80. $14,410.80 - $14,063.40 = $347.40 loss)			
	(Solutions To April 5 Memo)			
Mar. 31	Foreign Exchange Loss		96.15	
	Accounts Payable/Gustav, Inc.			96.15
	(15,000 Austria schillings x .08944 = $1,341.60 purchase amount. 15,000			

	Austria schillings x .09585 = $1,437.75 March 31 amount.				
	$1,437.75 − $1,341.60 = $96.15 loss)				
Mar. 31	Accounts Payable/Treynor, Inc.		14.78		
	Foreign Exchange Gain			14.78	
	(388,000 Hungary forints x .0129166 = $5,011.64 purchase amount. 388,000				
	Hungary forints x .0128785 = $4,996.86 March 31 amount.				
	$5,011.64 − $4,996.86 = $14.78 gain)				
Mar. 31	Foreign Exchange Loss		213.97		
	Accounts Receivable/Korosaki Company			213.97	
	(675,000 Japanese yen x .008210 = $5,541.75 sales amount. 675,000				
	Japanese yen x .007893 = $5,327.78 March 31 amount.				
	$5,541.75 − $5,327.78 = $213.97 loss)				

	International Journal				Page 5
Date	Description	Post Ref.	Debit	Credit	
Mar. 31	Accounts Receivable/Wyndham Company		144.00		
	Foreign Exchange Gain			144.00	
	(40,000 Australian dollars x .7609 = $30,406.00 sales amount. 40,000				
	Australian dollars x .7645 = $30,580.00 March 31 amount.				
	$30,580.00 − $30,406.00 = $144.00 gain)				
Mar. 31	Accounts Payable/Pokeva Company		33.99		
	Foreign Exchange Gain			33.99	
	(11,000 Finland markkas x.22185 = $2,440.35 purchase amount. 11,000				
	Finland markkas x.21876 = $2,406.36 March 31 amount.				
	$2,440.35 − $2,406.36 = $33.99 gain)				

28

EXAMS

Two exams are provided in this instructor's manual to measure student comprehension and performance.

Training Exam

The training exam covers material presented in the training manual portion of the practice set. It is designed to be administered after students have completed the training manual and before they complete the simulation. It measures the student's comprehension of international business and international accounting practices.

Performance Review

The performance review is designed to measure the student's performance in the simulation portion of the practice set. This test calls for the student to provide answers from transactions recorded and activities performed in the simulation. It provides a way for the instructor to check the student's performance without checking each individual activity in the simulation.

TRAINING EXAM

Write your answers on the answer sheet provided.

30 Points

1. The difference between a country's exports and its imports is called the _____. (A) Trade Surplus (B) Trade Deficit (C) Balance of Payments (D) Balance of Trade
2. If a country's exports exceed its imports, a _____ results. (A) Trade Surplus (B) Trade Deficit (C) Positive Balance of Payments (D) Negative Balance of Payments
3. It is called _____ when a company locates wholesalers and distributors in a foreign country and sells its goods directly to them. (A) Subsidiary Marketing (B) Direct Exporting (C) Licensing (D) Indirect Exporting
4. It is called _____ when a company contracts to allow a

foreign company to use its highly-recognizable name or business procedures to operate their own business in the foreign country according to the originating company's plan. (A) Licensing (B) A Joint Venture (C) Franchising (D) Contract Manufacturing

5. A company might enter a foreign market by establishing its own sales organization in that country and by having its goods manufactured locally according to its specifications by a producer called a _____. (A) Marketing Subsidiary (B) Contract Manufacturer (C) Wholly Owned Subsidiary (D) Licensee

6. A distribution center established in a foreign country, staffed with local employees and supervised by the company's managers, to distribute the company's goods in that country, is called a _____. (A) Marketing Subsidiary (B) Wholly Owned Subsidiary (C) Franchise (D) Joint Venture

7. Entering a foreign market by forming a partnership with a company in that country to manufacture and/or market the company's products is called a _____. (A) Franchise (B) License (C) Contract Subsidiary (D) Joint Venture

8. A company that enters a foreign market by building a new manufacturing plant or by buying an existing one that it operates is said to have established a/an _____ in the foreign country. (A) Infrastructure (B) Licensed Subsidiary (C) Marketing Subsidiary (D) Wholly Owned Subsidiary

9. The value of a country's currency, stated in terms of another country's currency for which it can be traded is called the _____. (A) Denominated Currency (B) Select Quote (C) Currency Exchange Rate (D) Currency Trade Rate

10. When an American dollar can be exchanged for more of a foreign currency and can purchase more goods in a foreign country, it is called a _____. (A) Negative Balance of Payments (B) Strong Dollar (C) Weak Dollar (D) Remeasurement

11. Steps taken by governments to protect their domestic industries and companies from foreign competitors so their domestic companies can survive and thrive are called _____. (A) Repatriation (B) Expropriation Without Reimbursement (C) Trade Protectionism (D) Retaliation

12. A tax imposed by a country on imported goods is called a/an
_____. (A) Tariff (B) Embargo (C) Import Subsidy
(D) Repatriation

13. A/an _____ prohibits a certain type of goods from
being imported into a country or from being exported from a
country. (A) Tariff (B) Import/Export Quota (C) Dumping
(D) Embargo

14. Direct or indirect payments made by a government to its
domestic companies involved in exporting goods so the domestic company can sell its goods at a lower price in foreign
markets and still earn a profit are called _____. (A) Dumping (B) Export Subsidies (C) Import Subsidies (D) Protective
Tariffs

15. Groups of countries with similarities and common interests
that join together to form trade alliances are called _____.
(A) Cartels (B) OPECS (C) Conglomerates (D) Economic
Communities

16. An organization of countries that produce a raw material or
commodity such as coffee or sugar and which controls the
supply and prices of those materials is called a/an _____.
(A) OPEC (B) Cartel (C) Economic Community (D) Trade
Association

17. The trade alliance of Belgium, Denmark, France, Germany,
Spain, the United Kingdom, and six other neighboring countries is called the _____. (A) European Free Trade Association (B) European Integration Association (C) European
Community (D) Central Market

18. To which three countries does Karissa Jean's export jeans from
the Denver office? (A) Japan, Canada, Australia (B) Japan,
Mexico, Austria (C) France, Germany, Greece (D) Japan, Canada, France

19. In what currency does Karissa Jean's France record its financial
transactions? (A) American dollar (B) French franc (C) German
mark (D) Japanese yen

20. The direct quote for British pounds is 1.6930 and the indirect
quote is .5907. How many American dollars can 20,000 British pounds be converted to? (A) 33,860 (B)11,814 (C) 20,000
(D) 22,837

21. The direct quote for French francs is .19337 and the indirect quote is 5.1715. How many French francs can 12,000 American dollars be converted to? (A) 2,320.44 (B) 62,058.00 (C) 12,000.00 (D) 32,189.22

22. The direct quote of Japanese yen is .008100 and the indirect quote is 123.45. The direct quote of German marks is .6597 and the indirect quote is 1.1518. How many German marks can 80,000 Japanese yen be converted to? (A) 6,515.20 (B) 427.49 (C) 11,375,176.80 (D) 746.37

23. An American company sold goods on account to a Mexican company for $14,500 (American dollars). The American dollar is the denominated currency. The direct quote for the Mexican peso is .3207 and the indirect quote is 3.118. The American company should record this sale by debiting accounts receivable and crediting sales for _____. (A) $4,650.14 (B) $45,211.00 (C) $14,500.00 (D) $24,930.58

24. An American company sold goods on account to a Canadian company for 20,000 Canadian dollars. The Canadian dollar is the denominated currency. The direct quote for the Canadian dollar is .8389 and the indirect quote is 1.1920. The American company should record this sale by debiting accounts receivable and crediting sales for _____. (A) $16,778 (B) $20,000 (C) $20,309 (D) $23,840

25. On August 5, an American company sold goods on account to a Danish company for $8,000 (American dollars), with payment to be made on September 5. The American dollar is the denominated currency. On August 5, the direct quote of the Danish krone is .1645 and the indirect quote is 6.0800. On September 5, the direct quote of the Danish krone is .1581 and the indirect quote is 6.3248. When the American company receives payment on September 5, it should recognize a/an _____ of _____. (A) Exchange Gain, $51.20 (B) Exchange Loss, $51.20 (C) Exchange Loss, $1,958.40 (D) No Exchange Gain or Loss

26. On August 6, an American company purchased goods on account from a Swedish company for 40,000 Swedish kronor. The krona is the denominated currency. Payment is to be made September 6. On August 6, the direct quote of the Swedish

krona is .1756 and the indirect quote is 5.6935. On September 6, the direct quote of the krona is .1808 and the indirect quote is 5.5300. When the American company makes payment on September 6, it should recognize a/an _____ of _____. (A) Exchange Gain, $208 (B) Exchange Loss, $208 (C) Exchange Loss, $6,540 (D) No Exchange Gain or Loss

27. On August 7, an American company purchased goods on account from an Irish company for 15,000 Irish punt. The punt is the denominated currency. Payment is to be made September 7. On August 7, the direct quote of the Irish punt is 1.7350 and the indirect quote is .5705. On September 7, the direct quote of the Irish punt is 1.6934 and the indirect quote is .5905. When the American company makes payment on September 7, it should recognize a/an _____ of _____. (A) Exchange Gain, $624.00 (B) Exchange Gain, $2,452.50 (C) Exchange Loss, $624.00 (D) No Exchange Gain or Loss

28. On June 20, an American company purchased goods on account from a British company for 5,000 pounds, with payment to be made on July 20. The British pound is the denominated currency. The American company's accounting period ends on June 30. On June 20, the direct quote for the British pound was 1.7397 and the indirect quote was .5748. On June 30, the direct quote for the pound was 1.7213 and the indirect quote was .5810. The June 30 adjusting entry for this unsettled account should be a debit to _____ and a credit to _____ for $_____. (A) Foreign Exchange Loss, Accounts Payable, $31.00. (B) Foreign Exchange Loss, Accounts Payable, $92.00. (C) Accounts Payable, Foreign Exchange Gain, $31.00 (D) Accounts Payable, Foreign Exchange Gain, $92.00

29. When translating foreign income statement items from a foreign currency to American dollars, the _____ currency exchange rate should be used. (A) Current (B) Historical (C) Weighted-Average (D) Adjusted

30. When translating foreign balance sheet asset and liability amounts from a foreign currency to American dollars, the _____ currency exchange rate should be used. (A) Current (B) Historical (C) Weighted-Average (D) Adjusted

TRAINING EXAM

Answer Sheet

Write your answers on the lines below:

1. _____	16. _____
2. _____	17. _____
3. _____	18. _____
4. _____	19. _____
5. _____	20. _____
6. _____	21. _____
7. _____	22. _____
8. _____	23. _____
9. _____	24. _____
10. _____	25. _____
11. _____	26. _____
12. _____	27. _____
13. _____	28. _____
14. _____	29. _____
15. _____	30. _____

KARISSA JEAN'S
PERFORMANCE REVIEW

Write your answers on the answer sheet provided.

25 Points

Locate answers to the following questions in the transactions you recorded and activities you performed as an international accountant for Karissa Jean's.

1. From the January 18 memo, what was the estimated cost in American dollars of Karissa's lodging in Lisbon, Portugal?
2. From the January 18 memo, what was the estimated total cost in American dollars for Karissa's trip, excluding air fare?
3. On January 9, Karissa Jean's purchased samples on account from CIA Mexicana Company. What was the amount of the purchase in American dollars?
4. On January 11, Karissa Jean's purchased samples on account from Cheung Wan, Ltd. What was the amount of the purchase in American dollars?
5. On January 15, Karissa Jean's sold jeans on account to Newton-John, Ltd. What was the amount of the sale in American dollars?
6. On January 17, Karissa Jean's sold jeans on account to Trans-World, Inc. What was the amount of the sale in American dollars?
7. On January 22, you were asked to write a memo to new employee Spence Blakeslee describing the process for preparing a retained earnings statement. On the retained earnings statement you prepared as an example, what was the November 30 retained earnings amount in francs?
8. On January 29, you were asked to translate a letter received from Gregorio Lamente from Spanish to English. In the letter, what product does Mr. Lamente say he currently imports to Mexico from the United States? (Give your English translation.)
9. On February 9, Karissa Jean's made payment to CIA Mexicana Company. What was the amount of cash paid?

10. On February 11, Karissa Jean's made payment to Cheung Wan, Ltd. on account. What was the amount of foreign exchange gain or loss that was recorded? (Indicate gain or loss)

11. On February 15, payment was received on account from Newton-John, Ltd. What was the amount of cash received?

12. On February 16, Karissa Jean's made payment to Takatsu, Ltd. on account. What was the foreign exchange gain or loss that was recorded? (Indicate gain or loss)

13. On February 17, payment was received from Trans-World, Inc. on account. What was the amount of cash received?

Questions 14-18 refer to the March 8 memo received from Sean McMasters of Karissa Jean's France asking you to audit the Karissa Jean's France general journal.

14. What was the correct amount of sales to Aschaffenburger GMBH on February 1?

15. What was the correct amount owed to Basballe, Inc. on February 4 for the purchase of office equipment?

16. What was the correct amount of foreign exchange gain or loss recorded in the March 1 receipt of payment from Aschaffenburger GMBH? (Indicate gain or loss)

17. What was the correct amount paid to Piazzolla SPA on March 2?

18. What was the correct amount of foreign exchange gain or loss recorded in the March 4 payment to Basballe, Inc? (Indicate gain or loss)

19. On the March 16 memo, you were asked to make calculations on a proposed system to eliminate foreign exchange gains or losses. On the fourth item, for a purchase for 20,000 Canadian dollars, what was the amount of net interest income or expenses? (Indicate income or expense)

20. In the March 31 adjusting entry for unsettled accounts, what was the foreign exchange gain or loss recognized for the sale made to Gustav, Inc.? (Indicate gain or loss)

21. In the March 31 adjusting entry for unsettled accounts, what was the foreign currency gain or loss recognized for the sale to Pokeva Company? (Indicate gain or loss)

Questions 22-25 refer to the April 11 memo asking you to translate the Karissa Jean's France financial statements from francs to American dollars. Refer to your translated financial statements for the answers.

22. What is the March 31 translated retained earnings amount?
23. What is the translated net income for the three months ending March 31?
24. What is the translated total assets amount on March 31?
25. What is the translation adjustment that was added or subtracted on the March 31 balance sheet? (Indicate added or subtracted)

KARISSA JEAN'S PERFORMANCE REVIEW

Answer Sheet

Write your answers on the lines below:

1. _____	14. _____
2. _____	15. _____
3. _____	16. _____
4. _____	17. _____
5. _____	18. _____
6. _____	19. _____
7. _____	20. _____
8. _____	21. _____
9. _____	22. _____
10. _____	23. _____
11. _____	24. _____
12. _____	25. _____
13. _____	

ANSWERS

TRAINING EXAM
Answer Sheet

Write your answers on the lines below:

1.	D	16.	B
2.	A	17.	C
3.	B	18.	A
4.	C	19.	B
5.	B	20.	A
6.	A	21.	B
7.	D	22.	D
8.	D	23.	C
9.	C	24.	A
10.	B	25.	D
11.	C	26.	B
12.	A	27.	A
13.	D	28.	D
14.	B	29.	C
15.	D	30.	A

KARISSA JEAN'S
PERFORMANCE REVIEW
Answer Sheet

Write your answers on the lines below:

1.	$179.43	14.	34,118.66 Francs
2.	$3,135.58	15.	3,025.33 Francs
3.	$1,923.60	16.	432.10 Francs Loss
4.	$413.89	17.	16,352.00 Francs
5.	$11,858.55	18.	21.31 Francs Gain
6.	$14,410.80	19.	$178.06 Expense
7.	3,418,775 francs	20.	$96.15 Loss
8.	Housewares	21.	$33.99 Gain
9.	$1,956.60	22.	$616,997
10.	$7.01 Gain	23.	$222,078
11.	$12,274.35	24.	$1,114,037
12.	$11.34 Loss	25.	$63,066 Added
13.	$14,063.40		